When We Were Shadows

"(A) perfect choice for school libraries... *When We Were Shadows* will inform readers, young and old, on the journey of a young boy during the Holocaust, but ultimately it will inspire all to discover how the human spirit can triumph over evil. Highly recommended."

- CM: Canadian Review of Materials

"This is more than an account of one boy's wartime experience. It is a story of human resilience, the power of family, and the kindness of strangers even in the most extreme situations."

- Rona Altrows, author of *At This Juncture*

A Holocaust Remembrance Book for Young Readers

WHEN WE WERE SHADOWS

JANET WEES

Second Story Press

Library and Archives Canada Cataloguing in Publication

Wees, Janet, author
When we were shadows / Janet Wees.

ISBN 978-1-77260-061-2 (softcover)

1. Jewish children in the Holocaust--Biography--Juvenile literature.
2. Hidden children (Holocaust)--Netherlands--Biography--Juvenile
literature. 3. Holocaust, Jewish (1939-1945)--Juvenile literature. I. Title.

D804.48.W44 2018   j940.53'18092   C2017-906506-8

Printed and bound in Canada

*Second Story Press gratefully acknowledges the support of the Ontario Arts Council
and the Canada Council for the Arts for our publishing program. We acknowledge the
financial support of the Government of Canada through the Canada Book Fund.*

ONTARIO ARTS COUNCIL
CONSEIL DES ARTS DE L'ONTARIO
an Ontario government agency
un organisme du gouvernement de l'Ontario

Canada Council   Conseil des Arts
for the Arts   du Canada

Funded by the Government of Canada
Financé par le gouvernement du Canada

MIX
Paper from
responsible sources
FSC
www.fsc.org FSC® C004071

Published by
SECOND STORY PRESS
20 Maud Street, Suite 401
Toronto, ON M5V 2M5
www.secondstorypress.ca

FOR ZE'EV

Dedicated to all the people and their families in Holland who risked their lives to save lives. And to all those whose families were part of the Underground/Resistance, a huge thank you for your sacrifices.

"Whoever rescues a single life earns as much merit as though he had rescued the entire world." —The Talmud

Because you have been where you have been
And I am now where I am now,
I will never be able completely to be
Where you have been,
And you will never be able completely to be
Where I am now.
But we can tell each other the story
And that will be enough.

—Awraham Soetendorp

(translated from Dutch and used with kind permission from Awraham Soetendorp)

Prologue
MAY 8, 1995

My dearest granddaughter Jenny,

For years you've asked me about my experiences during World War II. I haven't told you much because I felt you were too young to understand the horror and fear we lived with during those times.

I realize that you're now mature enough to hear my whole story. You've heard parts about how we lived in the Netherlands—in Den Haag, and then in Nunspeet. You knew we were hidden and eventually saved, but I'm now giving you the details of those years, including the letters I wrote to my *oma*—my grandma—and others.

Having me write letters was a trick used by my mother to keep me quiet during the days when I couldn't go to school, or when we had to whisper all the time. Like you, I was talkative, curious, and independent. Only when my imagination was engaged and I was writing, could I focus.

When Oma died after the war, I went through her belongings. In an old trunk at the foot of her bed, I found all my letters, tied neatly into bundles, ragged from being read over and over. I had written them on paper bags, notepaper, old receipts, pages torn from books, and wrapping paper from food deliveries. I took what the Underground brought me, wrote the letters, folded them up, and gave them back to the Underground to deliver to Oma. They didn't look fancy, but the stories inside made them come alive.

Jenny, here is my gift to you—my story, told with the help of those letters, about my childhood, long hidden in memories.

CHAPTER ONE
THE LEAVING

The first thing I remember from that time was someone shaking me and calling my name.

"Walter, wake up! Walter!"

I opened my eyes and saw my mother's face close to mine. Her eyes were overflowing with tears, and her hands were shaking.

"Hurry. You have to get dressed. I've put your clothes on the bed. Wear all of them. If you need help, ask your sister." Then my mother turned and left our room.

My sister was sobbing as she stuffed clothing into her rucksack. Hannah looked fatter than she had the day before. She wore a long skirt with a short skirt on top. Blue cuffs emerged from under the sleeves of her white sweater and she had on two pairs of socks—blue ones and red ones. At the foot of the bed I saw my rucksack bulging at the seams and next to it a pile of clothing—two shirts, two sweaters, two pants, two underpants, two pairs of socks. Confused, I began to dress myself in layers.

"Hannah, what's happening? Why are you crying? Why is Mama crying? Why are we packing? Why do I have to wear all these clothes?"

"We're leaving Zwickau for the Netherlands. We have to catch the early train," she said, her voice thick with tears. "Hurry and get dressed." Her back was to me, but I saw her shoulders shaking, and she was sniffling into her sleeve.

Oh, I thought, *a train! How exciting*! I'd only heard the whistles of the trains as they entered our city and only seen photographs of them in magazines. Now I was going to travel for real in a shiny black train that would hiss, whistle, and clank.

I was only five and a half. Hannah was four years older, so she helped me button my shirts and pull one pair of pants on over the other. She had to tie my shoes because I was so padded that I could hardly bend over. And I was too hot.

Hannah handed me my rucksack and told me she'd packed for me while I was asleep.

"Did you pack Affe?" Oma had made a stuffed sock monkey for me when I was a baby, and it comforted me. *Affe* (German for monkey) was always under my covers when I slept, but now it was gone. That monkey was my favorite plaything and went everywhere with me, especially into the kitchen when my oma and mother baked. I could smell yeast and cinnamon in the stuffing, reminders of home, and I wanted to take those memories with me.

"Yes, he's there," Hannah said. "Look." She opened my rucksack to show me Affe peeking out, jammed into a corner with legs over his head and arms akimbo.

"Now we have to go."

The kitchen was spotless, as if nobody had ever lived there. We all stood around for one last look. I remember Papa's lined forehead, and Mama's red braid peeking over the collar of her coat. Her eyes were red and watery. Oma's gray hair snuck out in wisps from her knitted hat, and she looked dazed. Her eyes were red-rimmed, above a straight line of a mouth clamped shut so hard that her lips disappeared. She nodded, distracted, as if someone was talking to her inside her head.

Oma had lived in that house most of her life. At the time, I didn't know the huge significance of our move because my parents sheltered me. I was to learn the truth three years later. It was an adventure for me when we left, even though everyone else was sad. I didn't know why, so I just followed instructions like a good little boy.

Mama gave me a piece of bread and some cheese to eat and helped me with my jacket. We crossed the threshold and left the home in Zwickau, Germany where I'd lived since my birth. Papa and Mama carried suitcases wrapped with leather straps. They both strained as they walked, tilting over to one side. I held Mama's soft, warm hand. Papa helped Oma with her satchel, which was small enough for her to carry. Mama and Hannah and I had our rucksacks on our backs. I felt like a wobbly Humpty Dumpty.

The sun was still asleep. As we walked down our road, all was still. The birds weren't up, and all of the homes were dark. Our steps on the stones crunched, and the heavy suitcases caused my parents to breathe heavily.

When we got to the train station, my throat caught. In front of us was a shiny black engine. Steam flowed from the top and hissing came from the wheels. My father helped Mama, Oma, and Hannah step into the compartment. A man in a uniform lifted me up and onto the train. He seemed to know my father, because he put his hand on Papa's shoulder and said, "Good luck."

We sat in two facing double seats. Nobody said anything. People slept in their seats with blankets and coats draped over their bodies. I wiped away the steam on the window and looked outside. Darkness surrounded us.

Once the train started, I could hear the clickety-clack of the wheels going faster and faster. The whistle sounded far away and our coach rocked from side to side. I removed my coat and one sweater. Mama unpacked some food from the small rucksack she'd carried on her back. We spread a cloth on the seat between Hannah and me, and Mama set out bread, cheese, and apple slices. Once I'd eaten, I fell asleep rocked by the motion of the train.

Suddenly I was shaken again. "Put on your sweater and jacket," Mama said.

"We're changing trains in Leipzig. We have to stay together and hold each other's hands," said Papa.

I'd never heard of this place before but I had no time to think about what excitement waited at the station. We had to hurry. And remember, Jenny, I was roly-poly with all my clothing, so it felt as if I was being dragged by my mother while my feet flew over the platforms.

We left the train and walked up some stairs, across another platform, until we found a bench, where we waited. I wanted to ask many questions, but Papa's face warned me against doing that. His brow was furrowed, and his mouth was set with tight lips. He wiped perspiration from his forehead. I held my tongue, thinking someone would tell me what was happening, but nobody spoke.

The train arrived and looked just like the first one. Once more, we found seats facing each other, but this time the people around us were awake and talking and drinking from thermos cups. The car had a mingling of smells from coffee to pastry to cheese, and many voices from young to old.

Oma told me to look out the window for wild animals now that there was sunshine. Hannah read from her book. Mama knitted, and Papa read some newspapers that had been left on the seat. I looked out the window and thought about the life I'd left behind. It was all jumbled together—toys, books, rubber boots for walking in puddles, stones to throw, sticks to turn over stones, smells of baking from our kitchen, the people at the market where Mama and I went to buy food, my stuffed monkey who was my best friend, the sweet taste of cherries from the tree in our backyard, memories of my opa and his sweater that smelled of tobacco and sweat when he hugged me. I tried to remember his face but he'd been dead a long time. I dozed off and on, for what seemed like a whole day.

Suddenly Papa exclaimed, "We're in the Netherlands!" and the lines on his forehead disappeared. He grinned. Mama's face crumpled up and turned red. Oma woke from her nap. Hannah looked up, scowled, and continued to read. Even though I was little, I knew she was mad at Papa and Mama because she didn't want to leave her friends. She hadn't smiled or spoken to them the whole trip.

When we left the train I stood on a platform surrounded by suitcases, rucksacks, and a language I didn't understand. Mama grabbed my hand, and we began to walk. Coats swished in my face, hands and legs moved swiftly past me. I was in a jungle of people.

The date was April 29, 1937. I was almost six and about to experience a new childhood.

After escaping from Germany, Walter and Hannah couldn't know that their carefree years in the Netherlands would end with the invasion of Nazi soldiers in 1940. Soon after this photo was taken they would be forced into hiding if they were to survive.

CHAPTER TWO
INVASION

Germany invaded the Netherlands on May 10, 1940. This changed the lives of everyone in our country, particularly the Jewish population. I was only eight years old by then, so what did I know? I was younger than you are now, Jenny. But even though I was too young to understand, I was old enough to interpret lowered voices and urgent words. I heard these as signs of dread in the adults around me.

One day when I came home from school, my oma was no longer there. Mama said some men took her to a safe place where she'd be with friends until the country was free again.

"We escaped Germany so we wouldn't have to be under Hitler's rule," she told me. "Now the Nazis are here in the Netherlands, and once again we're not safe because we're Jewish."

"I don't understand why being Jewish isn't safe," I said.

"Some day we'll explain, but now you just have to do what we tell you. Oma's gone somewhere more protected because if we had to run, she wouldn't be able to keep up. She's too old to run anymore."

"Will we be able to visit her?" I asked.

"I don't know," Mama answered. "They didn't say where she was going, only that she'd be with other older people in a safe place."

"Are we safe here? I can run fast!"

Mama held me close and whispered in my ear, "I hope so, I hope so."

My carefree three years in Holland had ended, it seemed. I just wanted to play and read and help my father in his tea and coffee shop in Den Haag. Over the years we'd settled into Dutch life easily. Hannah went to school and made new friends. Father started his new business. Mama and I looked after the flat behind the store, and she taught me to cook and bake until I had to go to school at age six. When it came time for me to attend school, I was ashamed that I couldn't understand or speak Dutch very well.

Mama had kept me home at first because of the language problem. But I was such a talking, moving child that she finally decided I should learn the language by being with Dutch children.

I overheard her talking to my father. "Walter needs an outlet for his energy and he needs to be with other children. I can't get my work done with all his questions and demands. He's never going to learn Dutch from me because I'm slow learning it, too."

At first it felt like Mama was saying I was a burden to her, but the excitement of meeting new children chased away that feeling, and soon I was eager.

The first school was fun, and I did learn the language from other students. A teacher removed me from class every day and used pictures and word cards that taught me to read and speak at the same time. When I was seven, I began to attend a school close to Papa's store. The teachers were nuns.

On the first day, the nun who was my teacher started the morning with a prayer and asked us to close our eyes and bow our heads. Being Jewish, I stood alone quietly but didn't follow her directions.

"You didn't close your eyes," the nun said to me, after the prayer ended.

"Neither did you," I replied.

After that, Mama took me on her bicycle to a different school that was farther from the store.

Just before the Nazi invasion, talk of war and armies filtered down in snatches of conversation and translated into my play in the garden behind our store. I would set up barricades of stones and sticks for the ants and shiny black beetles that scurried through the dirt carrying food. I'd watch them stop when they saw me, but when I stayed absolutely still, they'd continue around the barriers. As rewards for the insects, I'd scatter breadcrumbs and sugar along their route.

Those ants and beetles were my imaginary troops, but I didn't want them to fight like real soldiers. I knew that was bad and caused much sadness. The insects were alive and I didn't want to hurt them. But my wooden soldiers were only toys, so I'd smash them together in imaginary wars to vent my frustration.

When I tried to talk to my sister, Hannah, about the whispers I heard, she'd say, "Don't worry. We're safe." Even though I tormented Hannah with tickling, teasing, and pulling her braids, she still looked after me. I trusted her because she was four years older and my big sister.

Because of the invasion, once again my childhood had been interrupted. At first the Germans seemed to think of the Dutch as "sort of German" because our Queen's husband was German, and we shared a border. For a while the occupation wasn't too hard on the Jewish population. There'd been Jews living in Holland for centuries.

My father's tea and coffee shop in Den Haag stayed open, and people visited and discussed politics and the future of our country. A stray cat would visit me, and I'd make toys with sticks and strings, with balls of paper tied to the ends. The cat came by because I'd feed her. Mama always wondered about how much I ate. She didn't see me put food into my pockets to give to the cat afterward. During the day, the cat would sit on the roof of a small shed in our yard. The sun shone on the metal roof and seemed to give her comfort. Even when I called her she wouldn't budge. She only came down to play and eat when I got home from school.

Then everything changed—quickly and unexpectedly.

We got our orders to move inland when the Nazis discovered that the Dutch didn't support them. All Jews had to leave the big cities and give up their businesses and homes. The whole situation was confusing for me. *Why did we have to move again? Would we have to run? What did moving have to do with being Jewish? Why did my friends at school get to stay in the city? What was wrong with us?*

Nobody really explained the situation to me, and I think that was because on the outside I still looked like a little boy. On the inside though, I felt like I was being stretched into an older boy before my time. The change was too fast and bewildering for me.

Papa said there was a summer home in Nunspeet. Summer was over, and the home wasn't being used by the owners. Besides, not many people were taking summer vacations anymore, so we would be able to live there until the war was over. One night before we left, the butcher, who had a shop next to my father's, came to our flat. The man was tall with a messy shock of blond hair that would fall into his eyes. He smoked nonstop while my father and he talked. He still wore his white apron over his overalls. I could see splotches of blood and small pieces of raw meat hanging on to the stained, dingy cloth. I expected his hands to be covered in blood as well, but they were smooth and shiny, with clean fingernails.

"This arrangement will help us both," he said. "I'm not Jewish and can keep my shop open. If I can also keep your shop open, then you'll have something waiting for when you return."

"I don't know when that will be," my father said. "There are terrible stories about the Nazis and what they're doing to the Jews. We may be deported and never be able to come back here."

When I heard that, a cold chill slid down my back. *Deported?* I knew that fearful word. My sister and I were hiding in our room, but listening and watching through a crack in the door. I grabbed her, and she gave my hand a squeeze.

"We can sign the papers," the man said. "I'll own your shop, but only on paper. When you come back, I'll return your keys. If you tell me where you're going, I can send you the income."

Papa looked at the man closely. He didn't know the butcher very well. This was a time when trust could be dangerous, but what else could my father do? The years he had spent building a business and making a home were important to him. We all hoped that the situation wouldn't last very long and that we'd be home in a short while. At that time, I didn't realize what a risk this arrangement was for both men.

I saw my father slowly pick up a pen and write on the papers. Then he stood up and extended his hand. The man shook my father's hand and then suddenly grabbed him in a hug. My father's head jerked back, and his eyes widened. His arms slowly encircled the man and hugged him back.

As the butcher turned to leave, my mother gave him a box filled with our silver heirlooms, porcelain ornaments, and photo albums, all wrapped in sheets. He'd look after our valued treasures while we were gone. He pointed to my mother's wedding ring and asked her if she was going to include it in the treasures.

"No," she said, as a tear rolled down her cheek. She turned and smiled at my father.

The man took the keys to the shop and our box, and left our house. We wouldn't see him again for five years.

The next day we packed again and said good-bye to our home. Before we closed the door to the store, I wrenched myself away from my mama and ran through the house to the backyard. I wanted to say good-bye to the cat. I looked up and raised my hand to wave, but... she was gone.

CHAPTER THREE
SETTLING IN TO A NEW HOME

I could smell the heather before I saw it. There was a huge field across from our new summer home in Nunspeet.

It was a dazzling white house with a face on the front. The two top dormer windows were the eyes, and the windows along the front were a toothy smile. The back door was cut in half, and we could open the top to see outside, but wild animals couldn't get in.

One of the farmers on our road gave me a cat that I named *Moele* (whiner) because she was always whining and complaining. She followed me everywhere and at night, she slept in the dry birdbath in the front yard. She must have thought that if she was there when the birds landed she could catch them.

I attended school in Nunspeet, but found writing to be too slow for the speed of the thoughts in my head, so I didn't get good marks except

The summer home in Nunspeet where Walter enjoyed his last days of freedom before going into hiding.

in maths. My writing was messy, and I left out words. The teacher told Mama that I had to slow down and practice at home. That was why I began to write letters to my oma later on. It was good practice for my composition and my handwriting. It also kept me quiet when we had to whisper all the time.

My room was where the dormer windows looked out onto the front yard. I had a big bed that I could jump on. It had a metal head and footboard and a patchwork quilt with pieces of thread hanging along the sides. Sometimes the threads rubbed against my face as I was falling asleep and startled me awake. There was a small table with a lamp beside the bed, so I could read at night.

Moele, the cat, followed Walter everywhere and endured a fair bit of his playful energy.

The ceilings were sloped and peaked in the middle, so it was a room for short people. Papa hit his head sometimes when he came in. Along the wall across from my bed was a low bureau with three drawers. All my clothing fit into one drawer, my books in another, and toys in the third—except for Affe. He slept on my pillows. I kept my room neat that way. The room was so big and empty that I could hear my echo.

The best part was the space under the roof. There were small doors on the walls beneath the slope of the ceiling. Crawl spaces ran along each side. I called them my tunnels. In one tunnel there were boxes with dishes packed in newspaper. In the other tunnel there was nothing, so it became my playroom and my hiding place. I spent a whole day clearing it of spiderwebs and spiders and washing the floor.

Papa found a lamp with a long cord, so I could read inside the long, dark tunnel. I built towers with blocks and carried up sticks and stones to make tiny buildings. Sometimes at night, I pulled my quilt, Affe, and a pillow in there to sleep. It was fun when the rain drummed on the roof, and trickled down into the eaves. This was the first place I went when I came home from school. It was my homework room, my playroom, my bedroom.

There were two rooms upstairs, so Hannah had her own bedroom, too. I wasn't allowed to go in there. She even put a sign on the door that said, *"Stay Out."* Mama and Papa had their room downstairs between the kitchen and the sitting room. I didn't go in there very often either, but their room got the early morning light, and I could see the glow under their door when I went down for breakfast.

Our house was at the end of a narrow lane, so we were the first people to see the sun come up. We were told the house was named *Zonnegloren* (sunrise). The field of heather was across the lane and I kept my window open so I could smell it. Next to the field was another house where a Jewish family lived, but we didn't know them. They stayed inside most of the time. Their house was called *Heidehoek* (corner house in the heather).

Papa came home upset one day because someone in the town got angry about his German accent. Papa had to explain that he'd left Germany, and Holland was now his home. He didn't add that he was Jewish. When I asked why, he said, "It's no longer safe, even here, to be Jewish."

That gave me something to think about, because by then, I didn't remember much about living in Germany. Holland was my home, and I felt Dutch. I wondered if I could be both Dutch and Jewish.

CHAPTER FOUR
NEW ADVENTURES

23 March, 1941

Dear Oma,

Mama says it will be good to write you letters so you don't worry. My writing will be schoolwork practice, and will keep me quiet for long periods of time. I can't write in German so if you have trouble reading Dutch, maybe there's someone who can help you. Maybe you can think of my letters as lessons in Dutch. Now on to my news.

We moved to another town in the autumn. I can't say where, or give you any hints. It is risky to say too much. We have a nice house, a garden, and a cat.

I have a new friend, Henk. He lives on a farm on our road. After school, we go off on adventures in the forest. Henk's mother gives us cheese and bread. We turn over rocks to find snails and worms. We climb trees and pretend to be pirates on a boat. We built a shelter under a tree using dead branches, moss, and straw. We sit on old rags and study for tests. When it snows, we put on heavy coats and sit in our cave.

One day we met a wild boar. That made us stand still. It lifted its nose to sniff. His little eyes couldn't see very well. We backed away and when we couldn't see him anymore, we ran. I ran faster than I'd ever run before. When we got to Henk's farm, we stopped and tried to breathe. We looked at each other and started to laugh. We ended up rolling on the ground, giggling.

I remember a conversation I had with Henk last November. We were in the forest in our shelter eating and studying. It was cold, and we could see our breath.

"Where did you come from before you moved here?" asked Henk.

"We lived in Den Haag," I said. I was picking dirt out of my cheese that had fallen on the ground.

"Why'd you move here?" asked Henk.

"My parents thought it would be safer," I told him.

"Why is it safer here than there?" Henk looked confused.

"We're Jewish and Hitler doesn't like Jews." I wondered what Henk would think of me now. I remembered, too late, what Papa said about letting people know we're Jewish. But don't worry. I trust Henk.

"Oh. So, what's the matter with Jews?" he asked me.

"I don't know," I replied. "I asked my father and mother, but they don't know either."

"You're the first Jew I've met," said Henk, "and you seem fine to me."

We went back to eating and studying. It felt good at that moment to have a friend like Henk.

Now I have to get back to my schoolwork. I will try to write more. I'm very busy. I wake up, eat breakfast, go to school, eat, study, and go to bed. The days are short and the early dark makes me sleepy.

I hope you are well.

Love,
Walter

CHAPTER FIVE
NO MORE SCHOOL

1 October, 1941

Dear Oma,

The Nazis made a rule that Jewish children can no longer go to school. Hannah's very upset. She cries all the time. Now she studies in the kitchen where Mama bakes and cooks. There's flour on the pages of Hannah's books, but she doesn't care. Other times she goes into her room and reads all day. Sometimes she goes for long walks in the forest. I ask to go along, but she says she wants to be alone. She's fourteen now and switches from crying to laughing and from friendly to mean all of a sudden. I don't understand her anymore.

I don't mind missing school. There were always problems with my handwriting and quiet work. At one meeting the teacher told Mama, "Walter asks too many questions."

"Isn't that what school is all about?" Mama asked.

"Yes, but he asks more questions than the others, and I'm too busy to answer them all," the teacher said.

I like learning at home better. Mama works with Hannah, and Papa works with me. I'm trying to make my handwriting better. Have you noticed any change? Papa is teaching me history with books from the library. We do maths from a book Henk snuck out of school.

One day I was walking down the road, and a farmer stopped me. I didn't really know him but I'd seen him in the neighborhood. He was on his wagon and he called down to me, "Are you looking for something to do?"

"What do you mean?" I asked.

"I could use a good strong boy to help carry my milk into the village and to help me on my farm."

"I'll have to ask my mother but I'd like to do that!" I said, and I ran home. Mama was in the kitchen. I told her what the farmer said.

"As long as you get your schoolwork done, the rest of the time is yours," she said. She looked at Hannah, and they both nodded. They believed it was a good idea. I can be talkative when someone's trying to cook or study, so I think they're happy that I have a job now.

For the past two weeks I've been raking hay for that farmer. I also rake hay for Henk's father. I climb up into the haylofts and throw down feed for the cows. I mix the cow mess with the garden soil. It was stinky in the beginning. I covered my nose and mouth with a kerchief borrowed from Mama, but I'm used to the smell now.

This week I got to milk a cow. I didn't know how warm the milk was when it came from the cow. I always think of milk as cooler.

Sometimes the farmer and I ride to town with two horses hitched to a wagon. My job is to hold on to the team while the farmer makes his deliveries. The milk cans are too heavy for me to lift. I carry the empty ones from the wagon back to the barn.

It's almost harvest. We're going to gather potatoes, corn, onions, and carrots from the gardens. Sugar beets grow in the fields, and we'll gather them soon. Mama gets upset at the dirt under my fingernails. I have to brush my fingertips with soap before supper. Sometimes I bring home potatoes or carrots, and then she's more relaxed with me.

I don't know what I'll do when winter comes. There's not much snow here, but there won't be any gardens to look after. I'll still have milk deliveries, but I might have to find something to do with my spare time. I can't do schoolwork all day. There'll be no more insects to visit except in science. I do have books to read. Henk brings two books from the school library. He reads one and gives the other one to me. When we finish, we switch.

I'm almost ten now. My old toys don't interest me much, but I still sleep with Affe, the sock monkey you made me when I was little. It gives me comfort, and I think about you.

Love,
Walter

CHAPTER SIX
STRESSFUL TIMES

During the winter of 1941, Hannah developed osteomyelitis, which is a bone infection. Jenny, my dear, you've seen how your great-auntie limps; it's because of her childhood disease. She had to have an operation and be confined to an isolation ward in the hospital. We couldn't visit her until her health improved. When she came home two months later, she was in a cast from her armpits to just below her waist. She had to stay in bed for many weeks, propped up by pillows. She couldn't bend over, nor could she turn without great effort.

When she finally left her bed, she had to sit on a pile of pillows, so her feet hung down. No more bicycle for her, and walking made her tired. Her excitement for reading and her love of learning had disappeared. My sister was no longer the cheerful Hannah I had known. She didn't even bother me when I did silly things like making faces or standing on my hands and wiggling my feet. She just sat with an open book on her legs and when she fell asleep it would slide down to the floor.

Along with the anxiety of Hannah's illness, there were also strained times when a member of the local police visited Papa. He told Papa to speak only with him, not to any other members of the force. When I heard that I wondered what secrets the two men were sharing. I discovered later that the policeman was warning us of upcoming Nazi raids.

The cigar man in the center of town talked with Papa, while I sat outside the store and drank cold tea. My parents went for bicycle rides in the forest. They never talked much to each other, until they thought Hannah and I were asleep. These mysteries kept me intrigued. It seemed that secrets lurked everywhere—in the shadows, in the air, in the whispers.

The other Jewish family moved from the house across the lane. There had been two parents and three small children under the age of six. Once or twice I saw the mother wheel a baby carriage down the lane with the two other children holding on to the handle.

We never discovered where the family went, and nobody else moved in.

Each day ran into the next for us, and we never knew what awaited us in the morning when we woke. Mama baked and cooked, and Papa would go to the village and buy newspapers. Hannah would read. I kept working for the farmers and studying in my spare time. I was afraid to do something new in case I might have to leave it in a hurry. I felt like I stood on a gangplank that was bending and threatening to launch me into nothingness.

A lump formed in my stomach and remained there. I called it the lump of longing: longing for the hugs we used to share, longing for my oma, longing to feel safe, longing for an end to the war, longing to grow up so I could do something. I'd go to sleep with a plan to dream about the good times in Den Haag, but many times I'd wake up sweating and scared. Helplessness cloaked me. I drew pictures of darkness, shadows, and explosions.

Our rucksacks were packed and ready at the door in case we had to escape quickly. My parents protected my sister and me from what the world was experiencing and told us only the basics about our situation. We might have to run. The Nazis hated the Jews. If we were caught we'd go to labor camps and be separated.

Playful days gave way to night terrors and fear of the unknown as the family prepared to move once again.

We had no idea about the rest of the world. If we had known, we'd have been even more afraid, because most of Europe had fallen to the Nazis. We only knew about the Netherlands, and that was scary enough. At night, Mama and Papa listened quietly to our banned and hidden radio, but shared nothing with us. Hannah and I were in the dark twice over.

CHAPTER SEVEN
LIFE BEFORE HIDING

I worried about what I'd do when winter came, but it turned out there was no reason to be concerned. I was busy every day from morning to night. Then spring arrived and there were more jobs to do.

During the winter months I helped the farmers milk their cows and carry the milk to the village. The cows were in the barns most of the time, so it was always warm inside. Even the short walk from our house to the farms made me shiver, but once inside the barns I warmed up.

The lofts were full of hay, and I'd throw it down to the stalls where the cows could eat it. The farmers let me taste the milk. To this day, I think there's a different taste when the cows eat grass in the summer but hay in the winter. Maybe that's just my imagination.

One of the farmers gave me some seeds to plant in our garden behind the house. By the end of summer we would have fresh carrots and peas from our own yard.

After I finished my early-morning jobs with the farmers, I'd go home and do schoolwork. When school was over for Henk, I'd meet him and we'd play. Over the winter I borrowed books from our neighbor Tante Cor. She lent me Jules Verne books, which were fascinating. They were all about the future.

Henk and I built snowmen and spent time in our forest cave. We still studied, but our cave also became our "office of inventions." There was plenty of talking but not much building. We discussed Jules Verne's inventions and tried to make our own new toys. Everything we made was really just something that already existed, but we had fun anyway.

When the snow melted, Henk and I played "submarine" with our toy boats and soldiers. Wherever there was a puddle or a pond, we would put our soldiers on the boats and place them underwater, pushing them along until they surfaced and attacked a village we'd set up with twigs. Henk and I were always soaked when we got home, and our mothers couldn't understand how we got so wet so quickly.

Both of us read *The Count of Monte Cristo* and made swords for fighting. We took turns being the characters and we'd duel with our homemade weapons.

Hannah perked up more once spring came. She learned to walk better with her cast and didn't sleep as much. She went to visit friends from school, and they came to visit her. They'd go into her room and close the door, so I couldn't listen. Sometimes I could hear giggles coming from behind the door.

Mama and Papa puttered around the house and went for walks. Friends would come over for coffee and sweets. Sometimes other families would come to our house for dinner. After dinner the adults sat in the kitchen and talked and the children were sent upstairs. Secrets were always floating about. Whenever I entered a room where the adults were visiting, they'd change the subject and discuss the weather.

I looked forward to the summer because Henk had a tent and he said we could take it into the forest and camp for a few nights on our own. I didn't know if Mama and Papa would let me camp overnight because until then, Henk and I had only slept in our own backyards. Besides, I was worried about wild boars invading our tent.

As it happened, Henk and I took the tent into the woods a few days after school ended for him. His father helped us set it up, and his mother gave us cheese and bread and blankets. We took pillows from our own beds and wore heavy sweaters. Our first night was our last night.

It's surprising what can be heard in a dark forest when it's late. During the day, we'd hear birds mostly, and wind whistling through the branches. But at night it was different.

That night there were no bird sounds, except for the hooting of an owl and an answer from farther into the woods. Hearing the *whoo-whoo* gave me chills. We decided we'd go outside and search for the owl. But when we looked through the tent's entrance, we could see many eyes glaring at us from the trees. We had our lanterns, and the light must have attracted the forest creatures. I guess they wanted to see what was going on in their backyard.

We retreated into the tent and tied up the doorway. Remembering the boar that we'd met months before, we wondered if he, or his friends, would come to investigate. Just then we heard a snuffling nearby. We sat there hanging on to each other, not daring to breathe until the sound went away. Then we grabbed our pillows, scrambled out of the entrance, and ran all the way home in the dark.

All the lights were out at my house when I arrived. Mama came downstairs carrying a lantern and was surprised to see me. I was shaking and cold and just wanted to climb into my own bed. The next day, Henk's father took down the tent. That was the last time we tried camping in the woods.

When Henk was finished with his school year, we rode our bicycles to the next town and met two girls he knew. Just like us—they liked bicycling, camping, building, and exploring. The girls wore pants instead of skirts so they could crawl along the forest floor. And they didn't worry about getting their hands muddy or their faces smeared with dirt. Henk and I taught them to sword fight, and they soon became better fighters than we were. The four of us built a raft to paddle on the pond, but it sank before we could use it.

We rode to the next village at least once a week, until the girls and their families went on vacation. I missed them. I was going to write a letter to the one called Sofie, but I didn't know her last name. The other girl's name was Dini and Henk liked her better. They were always telling jokes, and Sofie and I listened and laughed in all the right places.

My garden sprouted, and I ate the baby carrots, so there weren't many for the rest of the family. The weather was nice that summer, and I stayed busy with the farmers. They even told me to take some days off so I could have fun. That was nice of them, especially considering what was to come next.

CHAPTER EIGHT
THE HIDING BEGINS

24 October, 1942

Dear Oma,

Last night they came for Hannah! Not the Nazis, don't worry. It was the Underground. Because of her osteomyelitis she's still in the cast. They don't think she can run if we have to escape quickly. She can't ride a bicycle or bend down to hide in deep grass. They're taking her to a secret hiding place in a hospital. She'll be in an isolation ward so other workers won't bother her. If they think she's contagious, they'll leave her alone. Even when she no longer needs the cast, she'll keep it on to continue the fake story that she is ill. Only the doctor in charge and his wife, who is his nurse, will know the true story.

When they came for her, Hannah clung to Mama and Papa and promised to run fast if we had to escape. But the man from the Underground pulled her hands from their clothing and walked her to the door. I watched as he lifted her onto the seat on the back of his bicycle. Hannah sat very straight and hung on with one arm. She waved with her free hand, then covered her face. I could see her shoulders shaking as she was taken away.

I feel relieved that Hannah will be safe but I miss her already. I have nobody to tease and no braids to pull. She used to read me stories from her schoolbooks even after she couldn't go to school. Mama always says that missing school is the biggest tragedy for Hannah because she loves books and learning. School has never been as much fun for me, so I don't mind not going. Exploring the forest and the farms is way more interesting.

We aren't allowed to own bicycles but we do. We hide them in a shed in the backyard. During the day there are no secret police or soldiers. Papa says "yet," so it seems that they may arrive any day. People in the village don't smile anymore. They don't greet me with a hello, or a pat on the head.

There are more night raids on our village. We have to leave our house near the heather field and find places to hide. We don't know how long we can stay here. Papa is having secret meetings with other men from the village. I'm sent to my room, and even when I try to listen, I can't hear what they're saying.

When I'm in bed I imagine all kinds of possibilities. In my head I see soldiers hammering on our door and breaking it down. I hear their voices booming in the dark. Barking dogs and bright lights appear behind my eyes. My heart stops when I imagine being dragged from bed and pulled along the floor to the stairs. I imagine my head hitting each step on the way down. When I fall asleep I dream about Papa fighting the soldiers and being hit with rifles and clubs. One night I woke up when a dog started to attack Mama in my dream. It was so real that I yelled, and Mama quickly ran up the stairs.

We're no longer allowed to have a radio. Papa has one hidden under the floorboards. Even though I'm eleven years old, Papa tries to shelter me from the bad news.

"We have to do whatever it takes to survive, Walter," Papa said when I asked him what was going to happen next. "If you have questions, you can ask them later. When I ask you to do something, you have to do it right away, without question."

I think I'm old enough to know what's going on—it has to be better than what's going on in my imagination. I know Papa's trying to protect me but I feel so helpless not knowing what to expect in the days to come.

Last week the same policeman came again and told Papa that there was going to be a raid. After dark, we snuck across the road to the empty house next to the field of heather. As we were leaving, Papa moved a spiderweb above the door so that if someone entered our house he'd know. There was already a web above our door and he just pulled it down so it covered the doorframe. I was so proud that he knew enough to do that.

We walked, bent over and in the shadows. Luckily there were clouds to cover the moon. We took our rucksacks and put on extra clothing to keep us warm because it's almost winter. I was glad there was no snow on the hard dry ground to make visible tracks.

It was dark at the back of the house, but there was a door with glass in the window. Papa knew that if he smeared the window with soap, the glass would come out without making a sound. After pushing out the glass, he reached in and turned the doorknob. We entered and crouched inside, so we couldn't be seen through the windows. The house was empty. Papa put the glass back inside the window and taped it, so it wouldn't fall out.

It took a while to see in the dark, and when the moon came out the light streamed through the windows. Papa told us to go upstairs. That way, if the Nazis shone a light into the house, they would only see the ground floor. We climbed the stairs backwards, sitting on our rears and moving upwards. We were worried about turning our backs.

All night I sat on the floor with my back to a wall. It was in a small space that might have been where people hung clothing because there were hooks above me. I couldn't sleep. Every sound made me jump. None of us spoke. Papa used his hands to give signals, but when he touched my arm he startled me. Two fingers on my mouth meant to be quiet. A hand on the top of my head meant we were safe. A hand on my hand meant to be calm. Papa's hand was warm and strong and it did calm me.

In the morning before the sun came up, we went back to our house. The spiderweb was still there. We don't know where the Nazis searched, but our house had escaped until the next warning.

Oma, you are so lucky to be with other old people where it's safe. Nobody will tell us where they moved you, but a man from the Underground told me he's making sure my letters get to you. I hope I didn't scare you too much with my stories, but you know how my imagination works. I used to like listening to your scary stories. Now it's my turn to tell you tales that make you shiver.

I hope you're well and I hope to see you soon when the war is over.

Love,
Walter

CHAPTER NINE
WHISPERS

17 February, 1943

Dear Oma,

Just as we were finishing supper a few days ago, the local policeman came to our house and told Papa we had to leave right away. Nazis were going to search every home in the village that night—every home—even ours and the house across the road.

We didn't bother to put away our food. We took our rucksacks, threw on sweaters and jackets, and followed the policeman into the forest. My heart beat so loudly I thought everyone could hear it.

I looked for Moele in the birdbath, but she wasn't there.

The forest was large and dark in front of us. The path was familiar because Henk and I had our cave nearby. I'd cycled on this path, and it was also the way I took to pick berries and mushrooms. After about thirty minutes, we turned off the path and onto a new one with more undergrowth. I had to push branches in front of me, and the mud mixed with snow made me slip. My pack was getting heavier and I was tired. We walked for what seemed like hours until we got to a large shape. The policeman gave Papa a key and disappeared.

The shape was a caravan, parked on blocks of wood. Papa opened the door quietly and motioned for us to go in. He made sure curtains were pulled across the windows before he lit a coal oil lamp.

Mama opened the cupboards and showed me boxes of food and some dishes. There was even water in a pail by a stove. One of my books was on the table that folded out from the wall. When I looked at Mama, she shrugged and put her hands out as if to say, "I don't know how that got there." Then she winked.

This must have been where Mama and Papa had cycled every day for the past few weeks. I watched them ride into the forest and thought they were gathering wood and food, but they had stocked the caravan without telling me!

When will they realize I'm old enough to understand what's going on? I hear things and I talk to the farmers. They tell me things that are scary, about how people are getting killed and how Germany is taking over all the countries in Europe. It just makes it harder for me when I don't know what Mama and Papa are thinking or planning. I'm afraid to ask because they're upset, and I don't want to add to their worries. Not knowing makes me feel like I'm in a passageway with no light and no end.

Since coming to the caravan more than a week ago, we've had to whisper so we're not heard. I try not to make any noise during the day, but sometimes the sounds of the foresters make enough noise to cover anything we do. I nap a lot when I finish my schoolwork. My notebook is full of drawings and stories. We play games but have to pound the cushions instead of cheering when one of us wins.

People bring us food and water along with pencils and paper for my letters. I was embarrassed to ask about toilets because there isn't one in the caravan. I've learned to wait for night to use the toilet. I have to dig a small hole in the dirt and then cover it up when I'm done. If only the Nazis would walk through the forest and step into one of those holes! I would laugh and laugh.

My bed is up a ladder above Mama and Papa's. We need a lot of blankets because the stove is not lit overnight. That way the smell of smoke doesn't spread. In the daytime our smoke mixes with the smoke from the old trees the foresters are burning.

I keep imagining Moele will find us here. She's a smart cat, but I hope she doesn't come up to the caravan and scratch at our door.

I'll write more letters when there's more news. The man from the Underground said he'll try to get this letter to you, so you know we're safe. We're together and living on tiptoe, ready to run at a moment's notice. I miss you.

Sad and afraid,
Your eynikl *(Mama taught me the Yiddish word for grandson)*
Walter

CHAPTER TEN
IN HARM'S WAY

One night, just as we were going to sleep in the caravan, we heard an explosion and a whistling sound, followed by a large boom.

Mama and Papa shot up in bed and Papa said, "I think an airplane has crashed. The Nazis will look for the pilot, so we need to move."

We'd heard airplanes overhead over the last six weeks, but none had ever crashed or been shot down near us. I ventured outside with Papa and looked at the sky to determine where the plane's wreckage might be. We saw a red glow in the distance above the trees and showers of glowing bits that looked like fireflies.

"Should we go or wait for the Underground to come for us?" Mama asked.

"We'll wait for an hour and then, if no one comes, we'll go off on our own," Papa replied.

We sat in silence holding on to our rucksacks and sweating in all the clothing under our coats. Papa made sure there were no coals in the stove. I tried to think of nice things like the heather, Moele, working with the farmers. I was almost asleep again when we heard whistles outside.

Three men on bicycles were there. Each of us got onto the back of a bicycle and we all rode away. Small branches scratched my face as we rode through the forest, once again escaping into the dark.

I shivered in the cold air, and felt more lost the farther we cycled. *Would I ever be warm again? Would the next hiding place be our final one?*

We ended up in the village of Epe. The men delivered us to a house at the edge of town. It looked empty. A high fence surrounded three sides and the front windows were shuttered. No smoke came from the chimney.

One of our men knocked twice, then once again. The door opened a crack. A man peered out, our man gave him a piece of paper, and the space expanded so we could go in. It was early morning but inside it was as dark as the forest. I heard shuffling, so I knew there were others inside. Mama tripped over something that turned out to be a mattress.

Luckily a small skylight in the ceiling allowed a bit of light to seep into the room. When my eyes adjusted, I saw men, women, and children seated in groups around an immense space. All the walls of the connecting rooms had been knocked down to make one huge area. People sat on mattresses along the walls. There was a large table at one end with old wooden chairs. A teapot stood beside a plate of sliced bread on the table.

I looked at Mama and asked if I could have some bread. I was so hungry. The tea was cold, but I didn't care. Water couldn't be boiled because smoke coming from the chimney would be suspicious; the house was supposed to be empty.

There were fourteen other people living in that space. In one corner on two mattresses was a family with two children—a girl and a boy, both under eight years of age, but very subdued. Along the opposite wall a father and mother with three older children, who seemed to be in their mid to late teens, used three mattresses. An old lady was sleeping on another mattress. Beside her, a young family with twin daughters slept on two mattresses. The old woman was their grand-mother. When I met her, I realized how much I missed Oma. Luckily there were no babies. That was my biggest fear—being betrayed by a baby's cry.

The three families had been hiding there for one week and had come from attics where the homeowners were increasingly afraid of being caught. That first night our rescuers brought bread and some cheese for the next day's meal. Tea and bread were what we had for the next three nights.

None of the children were my age. So while I'd smile and say a few words to them, mostly I slept or read. Sometimes the adults would play cards and I'd sit with them. The younger children slept a lot and played with building blocks or board games. The older ones read and talked amongst themselves. We all whispered.

During the days, Mama and Papa had cold tea with the adults and discussed what they'd heard and where they'd been. Every night a man from the Underground would come to see how we were and would stay for a game of cards and cold tea. He'd bring our daily bread rations and put them on the table alongside the large revolver that he took from his belt.

Mama, Papa, and I shared two mattresses. I could reach out and touch the man snoring next to me; that's how close together everyone was. I tried to tuck the thin blanket around me so I wouldn't roll over onto my neighbor. I had to sleep on my right side because the man slept with his mouth open and his breath blew into my face. I don't think he'd ever brushed his teeth in his life.

On the third night, we were getting ready to sleep when the telephone in the house began to ring. The noise shattered the stillness of the dark. Everyone jumped. We'd been told not to answer the phone, no matter what. But it kept ringing, and Papa said it might be heard outside. Finally a woman yelled "Enough!" and picked up the phone. We all heard what came next.

"GET OUT NOW! NAZIS ARE COMING!"

Seventeen pairs of feet scrambled on the wooden floor. Mama grabbed my hand, we whisked up our rucksacks, and stumbled out of the house. We could hear engines rumbling up the street. They were very close.

Across the road was a big field of heather. My friend, the heather! Everyone dove into the field and lay flat, hoping not to be seen. There was no moon that night so it was pitch-black, and the rain that was falling made it even darker. I clung to the earth and dug in my fingers. My breathing seemed loud enough for the Nazis to hear.

Suddenly I heard brakes and footsteps running up to the house. Smashing wood and glass, and guttural shouting echoed from inside. I remembered what Oma said once, about how the Nazis didn't like to get their boots dirty. I prayed that they wouldn't come into the field that was getting muddier by the minute.

Someone shone a light down the road and over the field. Luckily the heather was high and we were low. A gun was fired a few times into the heather, and the rain began to fall even harder. I heard commands in German and boots on floors and steps. Vehicle doors slammed and wheels spun away in the mud. They were gone. It had all lasted maybe three minutes.

We stayed hidden all night. I was on my stomach in the downpour with the mud seeping into my clothes. I was afraid to sleep.

Just before dawn I felt people rise around me and saw shadows moving. I thought about Hannah and how lucky we were that she wasn't with us because she wouldn't have been quick enough to dive into the heather field. A feeling of shame swept over me at that thought.

Papa softly called my name, and together with Mama, we slunk into the grove of trees at the end of the road. Some lights were coming on in the neighboring houses and curtains were moving. We'd been seen, and Papa said we had to hurry.

He knew about a barn on a farm near our old summer home. We walked through the trees for hours shivering in our wet clothing. I felt like I was going back in time, back to where we used to live before we disappeared. We'd traveled in a huge circle and were back where it all began.

When we reached the farm, we waited to see if anyone was in the barn. Papa thought most of the animals would be out to pasture and it was too early for milking. We crept along the yard and tiptoed into the barn. Soon the farmer would come to milk whatever cows were left, so we had to climb into the loft and bury ourselves in the hay before he discovered us.

The hay inside was warmer than the outside air, and I covered myself so it would soak up the wetness in my clothes. I could hear the pounding of my heart. I was sure that if the farmer had a dog it would smell us. What if the farmer needed some hay for his cows? I was terrified.

When the farmer came in I could hear him raking the floor below us. I gently pushed aside some hay and peeked through the slats, but the farmer wasn't where I could see him.

Soon the smell of fresh milk rose to where we were hiding. My stomach gurgled. I'd never worked at his farm, but I knew what the farmer was doing without seeing him. All that day I dozed and woke and wiggled my toes in my boots as the man below us came and went. At dusk the farmer left the barn and closed the door, but we couldn't move in case he came back.

By this time, I felt the need for a toilet. I tried to keep it in but the pressure was too much, and I could feel the hot liquid soaking my pants and running into the hay. I felt so embarrassed and frightened that I wept. I had to stuff my arm into my mouth to stay silent. That night I cried myself to sleep.

As I slept, Papa snuck out of the barn to find our former neighbor so he could contact the Underground. Just before morning, I woke to the sound of someone climbing the ladder. I closed my eyes tightly and covered my head with shaking hands. I felt a tap on my shoulder and jerked violently. There was Papa and the man from the Underground who used to bring food to us in the caravan. I was ashamed to stand up because my pants were still wet. So I sat on the straw and listened to their plan of escape.

Mama, Papa, and I left the barn and walked beside the man who'd come on his bicycle to get us. He led us deep into the forest again, and soon we saw some of the people from the attacked house, walking silently alongside men on bicycles. We were still whispering. It seemed a natural thing to do.

Eventually we came to a clearing surrounded by tall old trees. The sun was rising, but it was still dark in the forest and the air was cool.

Mothers spread out clothing for their families to sit or sleep on. People pulled out dry clothing from their rucksacks and changed. Once we were settled, I went into the trees, removed my soiled trousers and underpants, and put on clean ones from my rucksack. I dug a hole in the dirt and buried those stinky pants forever.

That night we slept under the stars, but gradually the Underground found places to hide some of us. Every day someone else would disappear. I still felt the bubble of fear in my chest and I couldn't seem to stay warm. The night sounds of trains, owls, trees creaking, and twigs snapping kept me awake, so I often fell asleep during the day.

Papa promised someone would come soon and take us to a safer place. I wondered what I'd done to the Nazis to be treated like that. Why did I have to hide in my own country? The Nazis were the ones who didn't belong. What was it about being Jewish that was so bad? If I'd been older I'd have joined the Underground. Papa was telling me more by then and he said the people in the Underground blew up bridges, stole food stamps, and shot Nazis. I wished I could do that.

CHAPTER ELEVEN
LIVING IN THE FOREST

After five days in the forest, someone came to relocate us. It was late in the afternoon, and many of us were sleeping. At first I thought we were being attacked and had to run again. I knew I didn't have the energy to keep running. I just wanted to lie down on the cool earth and take the consequences.

Two men from the Underground were there with bicycles. Seats on the front and back carried the younger children. The rest of us gathered our things, stuffing clothing into our satchels and rucksacks.

We followed each other quietly, trudging along with our heads down, trying to tiptoe through the soft earth, heading to some unknown place. We put all our trust in the people leading us through the forest. Broken by our experiences, we were a silent, glum little procession. By this time I was used to nobody bathing. Our body odors melted into the other forest smells—pine branches, old rotting leaves, and pungent animal droppings.

Over the days I'd listened to conversations and discovered that people had lost family members who had been transported to "work camps." Some had seen their homes burned. Others had lived in dozens of places since leaving their cities and villages. Families were separated and hidden in secret places. Many didn't know if their loved ones were alive or dead.

Nobody smiled, not even the children. When we stopped to rest, the children sat with vacant eyes, staring into the forest. The adults spoke to each other in whispers and took turns keeping watch. The Nazis didn't like going into forests because they were afraid of snipers, but they'd fire their guns into the trees and spray the area with bullets from fire roads that cut through the woods.

After about an hour, we came to a clearing where a log hut stood. Forest workers used these to rest and drink coffee when they were thinning trees or clearing the underbrush. But it was no longer real coffee; instead they brewed acorns, chicory, or grains. Real tea wasn't available so herbs were used instead. *Teetabletten* was made with sugar (when it was available) and herbs from gardens or forests.

There were no forest workers in the area that day, so we stopped for a while and made some bitter but hot brew before resuming our journey. Eventually we came to a denser part of the forest. Through the trees I could see a lonely hut, a duplicate of the cabin we'd visited in the clearing.

When I saw the hut, I pulled on my father's sleeve and pointed.

"We're lucky," he whispered. "The Underground has somehow convinced the chief forester to move that single hut deeper into the woods, so that anyone escaping through the forest can have shelter."

"Won't he get into trouble?" I asked.

"The chief forester knows he has to keep quiet about what's going on. He probably asked his assistant to take apart one hut and move it farther into the forest, to be used as another rest stop," Papa explained.

I thought the assistant was brave because he, too, must have known the reason for the move. He could get into trouble, but he moved the hut anyway.

"How do you know about the foresters' secrets?" I asked my father.

"The people in the Underground are helping us make plans and they're working with the foresters," he said. "They have stopped thinning trees, so the woods will be dense and dark enough to hide the hut from view."

It felt good that Papa was sharing this information with me and my hopes soared. Perhaps he'd tell me more about the plans and treat me like a grown man. After all, I was almost twelve, on the brink of manhood. In just over a year, I'd be thirteen, Bar Mitzvah age.

The foresters' hut was small, and all of us had to move in. Slowly, our bedraggled troop entered the hut. Benches skirted the periphery, and in the middle were a small stove and a table with cups turned upside down on a large tray. Families claimed the hooks along the walls and hung up their few belongings. There was a window in the door and one on the back wall. Someone had left a pile of blankets on the benches closest to the door. People quickly grabbed the blankets and spread them out to claim personal space.

A box of potatoes and carrots was tucked under the bench, along with a big pot. Some of the men went out into the forest to bring back wood for the stove and within an hour we feasted on mashed potatoes and carrots. We ate out of cups and put our spoons inside when we finished to mark them as our eating utensils.

We slept on the floor that night, and in the morning someone brought a small tent that my father and I erected at the side of the hut. This was where Mama, Papa, and I would sleep. It was cramped for the three of us, but our body heat kept us warm. One night it rained. I reached up to touch the canvas above me because it was holding water in a dip. I thought I could push the water out, but that was a bad idea. It started a leak and we had to move into the hut. We slept sitting up in corners because there was no room on benches or the floor. Children were even sleeping under the table.

It was during this time that Papa, some of the other men in our party, and some members of the Underground began to develop a plan to remain in the forest. One night, much to my delight, Papa confided in me.

"The Underground thinks our numbers may increase, and we'll need more places to hide. This hut is temporary, but if we can build other shelters tucked into hillocks or camouflaged with tree branches, we might remain hidden for a longer time. What do you think?" he asked.

"Will we still have to whisper?" I asked.

"Yes," he said.

"Living inside a hill is better than living in a tent, especially in winter!" I said with a smile, thinking that perhaps I'd be able to study more insects that lived in the earth surrounding the new huts.

My father smiled back and gave me a hug. "I thought you might like it," he said.

I expressed a concern. "Won't the construction noise alert the Nazis?" I asked.

"The noises will be the normal sounds foresters make—sawing and pounding and chopping. Since these activities happen during the day, nobody will think it's unusual. The Nazis will think we're foresters because we'll all look like workers."

"Can I help?" I asked.

"I'd be happy to have you work beside me, as my right hand," my father said and he smiled at me.

The idea began to take shape that we would become residents of a future village, built into the hilly mounds of the forest, camouflaged and invisible to the naked eye—an encampment that would become known as The Hidden Village.

CHAPTER TWELVE
THE HIDDEN VILLAGE

16 June, 1943

Dear Oma,

This is going to be a lo-o-ong letter. I have so much to tell you. I can't tell you where we are, just what we've done. We built a hidden village in a forest! Today it's three weeks since we moved in.

Men from the town (I can't tell you which one) offered their services to build the huts and we assisted them, so the work went quickly. It felt good to be working with other men. I feel so grown up and strong. I take pride in my work and hope our little village will protect many people.

The group chose four quadrants of land with fire roads on all sides. The land was covered and hidden by thick undergrowth. We had to clear the area before we began to build. Those trees were cut into logs. Only enough trees were cut to clear space for each structure, so we are still surrounded by woods.

This sign marks the entrance to the reconstructed Hidden Village, now a historical site. Note the four quadrants divided by fire roads where the Nazi soldiers patrolled at night.

It was my job to go into the forest and find young pine stems. The men chopped tall thin trees from deeper in the forest to avoid thinning out our area. All of us dragged those logs to the site and tied them together with wire to make walls.

Wherever there were small hillocks, people dug deep into the ground and hollowed them out, reinforcing the inside with the wired log walls. Those shelters have only their fronts showing and are almost underground. From a distance you can't see them. The camouflage is excellent.

Some freestanding huts had to be built above ground because there aren't as many hills in one area as in the other three. Young pine stems were used to cover the outer walls made of thicker logs wired together to stand tall. One of the villagers, a roofer by trade, transformed heather into thatch for the roofs and walls. Happily we're in one of the heather huts. I remembered the first time I'd smelled the heather and how the scent would come through my open window. I began to daydream about our life back then. Papa had to shake me out of my thoughts because we were supposed to be working.

One of the in-ground huts of the recreated Hidden Village shows how solid and well camouflaged they were. Six in-ground and three freestanding huts made up the village.

The huts that are dug into hills have smaller windows at the front, and the ones above ground have larger windows. Every hut is different. Heavy dark cloth covers all the windows. We spent many days dragging logs, building walls, thatching roofs, and installing windows.

While we were working, women and children stayed in the rest stop during the day. A few other people who needed to hide were brought to the forest during those final days. They slept in tents and helped when they could. I really didn't get to know them. I was busy during the day and tired at night so I'd fall asleep instantly.

On three quadrants are two huts each, and three huts are on the last quadrant. We're not allowed to go on the fire roads, which are for fire-breaks. So ours won't be like a neighborhood in the city where we can pop in for a visit. Nazi jeeps drive up and down the roads on patrol every night. Little do they know we're here.

Let me describe the inside of our hut. Most have the same design with bunks lining the walls and a table and stove in the middle. I know this because I helped on all four quadrants. Now I'm restricted to our quadrant for safety reasons.

The inside of our hut reminds me of ships I've seen in books. Wooden stakes hold up the log walls. Beds are up-and-down bunks. The two longer walls have two bunks each, end to end, and the back wall has one bunk. There is a row of hooks for clothing in the corner. Ten people can live in each hut, but we've been warned that sometimes we may expect fourteen or more.

The floors are dirt. Once a week it'll be my job to bring in soft twigs and moss to cover the dirt. Some local residents may bring old rugs for the floor. In the middle of the room a small camp stove sits on the large table. During the day Mama and the other women cook on the camp stove, so the smoke stays in the hut. We have no chimneys so we open the windows to get fresh air. Papa says any smells that leave the hut will mingle with the forest smells. At night I write by the light of a gas lantern, which, at the moment, is getting lower.

This interior photo shows how cramped the living space was, even with most of the ten bunk beds missing.

We have no privacy. Shy people dress and undress under the blankets. We wear our daytime clothing all the time in case we have to make a quick escape. We're always ready to run. You can imagine how foul-smelling a small space carved from dirt can be with ten or more unwashed people.

For the first few days and nights I jumped at every little noise. Life is now taking on a routine. We sleep at night so our noise isn't heard by the patrols. The quiet surrounds us; even the birds sleep. There's always someone on watch in every quadrant, day and night, and we all know the signal to run. It's the loud whistle that people make when they put their fingers in their mouths to call their dogs or get someone's attention. I dread the time we hear that whistle.

Some nights, just before dawn, when we think the patrols have gone back to their base, Mama wakes me to go with Papa and get water. I sleep in an upper bunk because I'm small, and can crawl down a ladder. Papa and I walk to the well in the dark for washing and cooking water. A forest worker owns an old house nearby, and we use his pump. He ignores us when we fetch water. It's hard to be quiet walking through the forest in the dark. I can't see where I'm going so I hang on to a string attached to Papa's belt. Some nights I see shiny animal eyes watching from the trees. Eventually, a well will be dug nearer, and we won't have to walk as far.

We each carry two pails of water, for the two huts in our quadrant. I never realized how much we depend on water and how much we take it for granted. Never again for this boy!

We put water in a container with a dipper for drinking. Our cooking water is never thrown out. It goes into a big pot and is used over and over for more cooking. There's one pail used for washing clothes. The same water is used for everyone's clothes and then can be used for bathing. People string up blankets between trees for privacy and go behind them to wash. In case we're found, people usually remain half-dressed as they bathe. I don't know what we're going to do once winter comes.

Our toilet—a deep hole with a large tree branch across it for camouflage—is outside. When it gets filled, a new hole will be dug and the dirt will cover the old space and the smell. We go to that area in pairs, in the dark, looking for the tree with a white cloth that marks the spot. I worry that I might miss the flag and fall in. My thighs are getting strong from squatting! We keep watch with our backs turned to give each other privacy.

We talk about what might happen if soldiers come in the night and fall into our toilet holes. We laugh as silently as we can. Sometimes I have to cover my face with a pillow because I'm laughing so hard.

In our hut we have an engaged couple. He was a dental student and is continuing to study. She was a schoolteacher. An older couple was separated from their grown children when the Nazis bombed Rotterdam in 1940. They have been on the run ever since. A British pilot, who was shot down and injured, is waiting to get better and find his way back to England. There's also a German deserter and an escaped prisoner of war from Russia. They look interesting but keep to themselves. Papa can speak German, so he and the deserter talk.

The dental student is tall and skinny and teases his fiancée all the time. Every so often he checks our teeth to make sure they're healthy. His *nose is buried in his books because he leans so far down to read them. His glasses were lost when he escaped from his village. When he writes in his notebooks, he murmurs to himself.*

The dental student's fiancée is short and slim with red hair held back with ribbons. She has many different colored ribbons that she uses over and over. Sometimes the only reason I get up in the morning is to see what color her bow is that day. She's pretty, and when I look at her I feel my cheeks get hot. I wonder if anyone notices. She reads a lot and asks her fiancé questions as he studies. Their names are Alexander and Alexandra. I always mix them up.

I like to watch the older couple. She knits and goes to bed with her needles to use as weapons if we're attacked. What the man lacks in hair the wife makes up for with her long braid that reaches almost to her waist. The husband wears a tweed hat on his head because he has no yarmulke. He often prays, reading a tattered leather prayer book. His lips move quickly. Spit sometimes sprays the pages.

I remember Opa praying when he was alive, but I have never seen Papa do it. Mama and you used to light the Shabbat candles in Den Haag, and Mama continued in our summer home. That stopped when we had to run into the forest. Following religion on the run is difficult. Still, I feel comforted when I hear the prayers, even though I don't always know what they mean.

The British pilot is David. His leg is bandaged where he was injured. The dental student helps change the bandages because he's the only one with any medical knowledge. David has a British accent and is teaching me English. Mama says I'll sound like a Brit when he's done! It's interesting to see what goes on with the three military men. The pilot is on our side, the deserter was on the other side, and the prisoner of war has experienced both sides.

The other hut in our quadrant hid two American flyers who made too much noise and walked down the fire paths and smoked. They were rude and showed off as they walked. They wouldn't listen to Papa when he told them how dangerous it was. Everyone was nervous. Papa talked to our Underground contacts and the other day I noticed that one of the flyers was gone. He's been moved to another hiding place away from our village, and from now on, American pilots will be put in different quadrants. I find it easier to breathe knowing that.

Alfred is the German deserter. He's tall and heavy with blond hair that falls down his back and over his ears. His eyes are bright blue and could light up the darkest room. His face is hidden by a beard and moustache, so his eyes are more noticeable. For a large man his hands are long and slim. I wonder if he plays piano. He has hands like Mama, who loves to play.

Alfred was a sports teacher in Germany, and he leads us in exercises inside the hut. We run on the spot, do squats, and jumping jacks. It's so close inside that we do the jumping jacks one person at a time. It's become a contest to see who can do the most. Of course, Papa always wins because of his athletic background. Do you remember when he was a national champion decathlete representing Germany when he was just twenty-two? I bet *when he married Mama, you thought he'd be a pretty strong son-in-law.*

The prisoner of war is called Kazimir. He's shorter than Alfred but just as stocky. His rosy cheeks make him look as if he's just finished running a race. His curly hair falls in his eyes, and he always pushes it back. Mama says she should give him a haircut. He carves wooden figures and when he really concentrates, Russian words fall from his mouth, even though he can speak passable Dutch. Every night he goes to bed wearing his boots and two heavy sweaters, so he's prepared if we have to flee.

Kazimir's heavy sweaters remind me of Opa's sweaters and vests. I remember the smell of sweat, cooking, and pipe tobacco every time I climbed onto Opa's lap. Even though I was only four years old when Opa died, I can still feel how he nuzzled my cheek with his rough beard. He put me on his shoulders when we went for walks, and I felt like I was flying.

Kazimir was a farmer and also a truck driver for the Russian army. In 1941, the Nazis captured him during a sudden attack on Russia. He spent two years in camps in Germany and then escaped to Holland. Our village is his hiding place until the Underground finds somewhere he can continue the fight against the Nazis. At first he and Alfred didn't talk, but now they seem to be accepting each other. I was nervous that they might fight, and I tried to avoid them. That's hard in a small space. Luckily their bunks are across the room from each other, so they can keep their distance.

There are no children in the other hut on our quadrant. Except for that one remaining pilot from America, I don't know who lives there right now. In addition to David's English lessons, Papa teaches me maths and geography. Kazimir, the POW (that's what Papa calls him), is carving little figures out of the scraps of wood from the forest and says he'll teach me to carve. I read every day, and my letters to you are my writing assignments. We play word games and make up crossword puzzles.

I thought Opa was a loud snorer when he was alive, but he'd be drowned out by the other people here. Everyone snores. I lie awake listening to the symphony of snores, with different sounds at different times. I have to wear a hat to bed to cover my ears. Papa says not to worry about the Nazis hearing the snores. The fire paths are too far away.

Your grandson, feeling safer at last,
Walter

CHAPTER THIRTEEN
DAILY LIFE IN THE VILLAGE

13 July, 1943

Dear Oma,

Here I am again. I want to tell you more about what we do every day in our little hut. We are with people who used to be strangers but are now becoming friends.

People from the nearby villages ride their bicycles into the forest and bring us food—mostly potatoes, a little meat, and sometimes fresh cheese. We eat what grows in gardens or what's been stored in root cellars or baked in people's kitchens.

We're known as onderduikers—*people in hiding. Our village is called Pas Op. That's what the farmers used to say to travelers a hundred years ago—"go safely." Papa says he's heard from the Underground that there are thousands of Jews hiding in Holland in Dutch homes and barns.*

The Nazis kill anyone hiding Jews, so I have to be careful not to mention places and names.

Bathing and washing clothes doesn't happen much, so you can imagine how smelly it is in here. A few people don't worry about privacy anymore. When it rains they go naked outside and let the rain wash them. I don't know if I'm ready for that. Right now the rain is cool. Going back into a warm hut wrapped in a blanket seems to make it worthwhile to them.

Freestanding huts were not hidden in the earth but were covered with heather and greenery that made them virtually impossible to detect from the fire roads.

We hang our rucksacks on hooks near the door for a faster escape. Some people use their sacks for pillows. For breakfast and supper we eat bread and cheese when we have it. Sometimes we have boiled potatoes and other vegetables that come from local gardens. Our old friends come to visit us every Sunday. They pretend to be picking mushrooms. They tell us all the war news and bring food and identification papers. Those are for the injured pilots and escapees who'll be leaving soon.

There is a rumor that this couple is hiding a family of Jews in their attic and that they arrange for other hiding places in homes and farms around the countryside. They are our main contact for the Underground, kind of like bosses of everyone. We love and respect them and they always hug us when they visit.

So what do I do during the days? I continue to whisper and jump at every strange sound. For school, I read anything, including my Treasure Island *book. This must be my twentieth time. Every time I read it I notice something new. The pilot teaches me to read places on maps. Smuggled newspapers are read over and over. I've filled four notebooks with drawings and stories. Sometimes I play cards with the old lady or the fiancée.*

I'm going to write a letter to Hannah, but nobody can deliver it because it is dangerous. I'll keep the letter until I see her again. At least she'll have something to read when she gets home.

Every day is the same. Wake up, eat, go outside to the hole in the ground we call a toilet, spend the morning doing schoolwork on my bunk. On cloudy afternoons, Papa and I sneak through the trees searching for mushrooms, berries, and herbs. Now that summer's here, there are plenty. We go to areas with more trees and wear colors that blend in. That way we are harder to see.

Sometimes I develop projects. In my little garden in the forest I planted some potato "eyes" that hopefully will grow by autumn. I'm thinking about how I can invent a private place in the hut for bathing standing up. The design might work in the corner near the end of the double bunk. We have ropes strung from bunk to bunk to dry clothes; maybe I can get more rope and make a privacy curtain.

I feel lucky to be here because I know others aren't as safe as we are. I'm so thankful to our helpers who do what they can to keep us safe.

There isn't much more to tell you about. Our days are filled with eating, learning, sleeping, and fear—fear of tomorrow and whether we will all live to see it.

Walter

CHAPTER FOURTEEN
LETTER TO HANNAH

18 July, 1943

Dear Hannah,

I don't know if you'll ever get this letter. It's too dangerous to send to the hospital in case someone opens it. There's no reason for anyone from the Underground to visit you. So this will be written and kept until I see you again. I'm going to share more with you than I do with Oma because I don't want her to worry about me.

It's hard to imagine you lying in bed day after day with nothing to do but read and sleep and eat. I know you'll have some books. My memories of you are with a book in your hands. Remember Mama complaining "Always with a book!" when she wanted you to help her in the house?

Where we're hiding now is safe for the moment, but there's always that sense of dread inside that prevents me from believing that we'll survive this war. My days seem empty, even with schoolwork to do. I can't study all the time. I miss my ant and beetle armies from our backyard in Den Haag. I wonder if they're still alive making homes and carrying crumbs to their families. It was always so much fun watching how they went about their tasks and how they navigated around the walls I built for them. I try to mimic their determination, but there's always the nagging fear that no matter how many barriers I face, I may not find my way around them.

There are interesting people in our new "village." I try to talk to them but they seem to have dark secrets. They don't really respond to my gestures of friendship. One man, who lives in a nearby hut, was angry that a German deserter is living with us. Papa explained that the deserter is also a victim of the Nazis and would be killed if he were discovered. Our neighbor still thinks the deserter is a spy.

Alfred, the deserter, came to us shortly after we moved in. He was injured. He slept a lot and dug in the forest for mushrooms and berries that he shared with us. Sometimes I hear him yell in the night. I'm not the only one having nightmares. Papa showed him how to tie a rag around his mouth to prevent him from calling out in his sleep. The first night he slept with the rag, I thought he might stop breathing, but his snores soon proved he was alive.

The other stranger is from Russia. He was captured by the Nazis but escaped, and I know he has an interesting story waiting to be told. He's quiet and carves little figures out of branches and twigs. He's showing me how to carve, but I'm not good at it. When his shoelace broke, he used it to make a necklace for Mama with a wooden figure he'd carved. She wears it every day.

The dentistry student and his fiancée read a lot. He studies because he has hopes of graduating after the war and becoming a dentist. He says there'll be many people needing care because of the poor diets of wartime. He tells me stories about growing up and deciding to become a dentist. He wants to educate people before their teeth are already rotten.

The other day the dental student's fiancée was helping me with my schoolwork and asking me questions to exercise my brain. I felt brave enough to ask her why she couldn't teach in Holland.

"Because I'm Jewish I'm not allowed to teach, just as you aren't allowed to attend school," she said.

"Do you miss being in the classroom with your students?" I asked.

She looked off into the distance and a smile appeared. "Yes, I miss my class, but now you're my student, and we're both allowed to teach and learn in this village."

She and I develop crossword puzzles so others can do them for entertainment. Most of them get completed, but maybe I'll keep one or two empty ones for when you come home.

The older husband and wife sit on their bunk most days, talking about what used to be. Sometimes I sit with them and listen. It must be comforting for them to remember the good times. I like to remember the earlier days of my life, but I see only fear and hiding in my future.

I miss you a lot, Hannah. I teased you and got on your nerves, I know, but I love you and miss you. I felt protected when I was around you because you were my big sister. My worry about you in the hospital sometimes shows up in my dreams, which are more like nightmares. Papa tells me that you're safe and won't be caught. But you know my imagination; it runs wild sometimes.

Until I see you again and can give you a big hug,
Your brother,
Walter

CHAPTER FIFTEEN
CHANGES

12 September, 1943

Dear Oma,

The English pilot is gone! I woke up today and his bunk was empty. Papa says the Underground came to get him in the middle of the night to return him to England. Nobody knows how they'll do that. Papa says there have been documents stolen from bombed buildings and used to make false papers.

After the pilot left, Papa told me a big secret. David, the pilot, is going to deliver a letter to Papa's family in London when he gets back. Papa isn't sure they're still there because of all the bombing, but David says he'll search for them and tell them we're safe.

Did you ever meet Papa's family before they moved to England? I don't remember them, but I think they were very smart to leave when they did.

It was like they could see into the future. They must have sensed what was coming. Papa said he and Mama didn't leave with them because they thought we'd be safe in Holland. Nobody really believed the Nazis would become so powerful and dangerous.

Who'll come to our hut in David's place? I often wondered but was afraid to ask if he was the pilot of the airplane that crashed near our caravan a few months back. That night seems like a lifetime ago. My English is much better thanks to David. I'll miss him, but I hope he gets to bomb Germany even more when he recovers.

The Russian and German are still with us. I write stories imagining their adventures before they came to our village. If they ever tell us what happened to them, I'll see if I was right. Kazimir carves many figures of animals. He gives them away to the other hut and to the villagers who bring us food and information. He also learned to speak better English from David.

Sometimes Alfred, Kazimir, and I practice our English by play-acting. We pretend we're at a café and order food. Sometimes we ask for directions as if we're lost. We don't know if we are saying the right words though, because nobody else in the hut speaks English. A second American pilot used to be in another hut. He also helped with our English when he came to visit David. The two pilots had a lot in common, and it was interesting to listen to their stories, even though I didn't understand all the words.

There's nothing else to write about. Every day is the same. I don't want anything exciting to happen if it means we have to move again. So I'll just learn my maths, look at maps, read my book over again, write stories, and draw in my notebook.

Mama still tells me stories before I go to sleep. Affe listens in and so do the people in the other bunks. Mama says I should write my life story. But my life is only twelve (pretty soon) years long. What do I have to say? Mama thinks it's a good idea because it'll force me to remember the fun I had when I was a small child. She says it will take me to a place in my mind where everything is better.

The other night she started to tell me the story of when I was born. I don't remember of course, but Mama looks off into the distance as she speaks and seems to see the past unfolding before her. Maybe she should be writing HER life story!

Your grandson,
Walter

CHAPTER SIXTEEN
WINTER IN THE FOREST

Jenny, I've lived through many winters in the sixty-four years of my life, but the winter in The Hidden Village stays with me the most. The 1943-44 winter came, and with it fell snow that bent the trees surrounding our little community. Snow covered the plants we depended upon for food. Sometimes we had to pour salt down the pump to melt the ice that covered the water. I had the task of smoothing over our steps in the snow to make it look like animals had been there.

We made our own entertainment, and evenings were spent telling each other stories from the past—some imaginary and some real. Sometimes I could see people slipping into their own fantasies. Their eyes would look off into the distance, and small smiles would appear. Their bodies seemed to relax and their eyes would close as if they were dreaming. Every Friday the old man would say prayers at sunset.

I would lie on the bunk for hours imagining myself in scenes from books and movies I'd seen before the war. Being a pirate, beggar, sailor, orphan, or in a family that was rich with many children, living in a mansion somewhere elegant and peaceful—those were some of my favorite fantasies.

Memories of all the people in my life—classmates from school, my friend, Henk, from the summer home, teachers I liked, regular customers from the store who'd tease me—made me homesick. One recollection was of my father's friend Willie, from Amsterdam. He had a daughter who was so beautiful I couldn't look at her. Willie and his family were hiding because his wife was Jewish. The Nazis tried to recruit Willie, but he disappeared with his family overnight, leaving rumors in his wake. I'd imagine rescuing the daughter from wherever she was hiding and taking her and her family to our village.

We rationed our food because it was difficult for the townspeople to come with their bicycles in the deep snow. They had to be careful not to leave trails for the Nazis to see. Sometimes packages would be hidden on the edge of the forest and foresters would deliver them to us. One week it was so cold, I didn't get out of bed except to go to the toilet outside.

Ah, the toilets. We'd dug deep holes far enough away from the huts in the forest so the smell wouldn't give us away and so we couldn't smell our waste. My father had some lye he would scatter in the open- ing every so often. The holes were covered with trees and planks of lumber that were easy to move unless the snow was deep. Because of all the trees, not as much snow landed on the ground. It stayed on the branches, and sometimes we'd pull the boughs to make snow showers.

Going to the toilet was a major undertaking. First, I had to bundle up tightly enough to be warm but loosely enough to be able to remove my pants. It was a tedious undertaking and took a long time. I tried to make as few tracks as possible, and going back I used a broken branch to obliterate the footprints. One day, someone in our quadrant forgot to put the planks back in position and I almost fell in! I'm certain small animals perished in the cesspool below, but I never looked.

Our hut's population didn't change much. The English pilot left and an American took his place for about a week. The POW and the deserter left that winter, one at a time and totally unannounced. They were as unobtrusive as they could be in a small hut with ten people. One morning I woke up, and Alfred, the deserter, was gone. Tucked under my blanket was a letter.

CHAPTER SEVENTEEN

THE EMPTY BUNK — FAREWELL FROM ALFRED

13 December, 1943

Guten morgen *(good morning)* Walter,

Forgive me. I leave and do not tell you. It is for your safety. Your mama helps me write this letter because my Dutch is not so good.

In Germany I was teacher in Cologne. I was married, with young daughter. Cologne was bombed in May, 1942. I was in army. To this day, I do not know fate of my family.

The German army send me to island in north of Holland for my last post. I use anti-aircraft guns. Sand dunes become bunkers to shoot British airplanes flying to bomb Germany.

I feel depressed because I have no family news. I listen to BBC to hear the Allies' side. My comrades laugh. I believe BBC. Stories about the treatment of Jews upset me. I decide Hitler must be stopped. I feel ashame.

Dutch people living on the island avoid us. They cross street when we walk on same side. They cycle away from us. They do not enter cafés if we are inside. Every night I sleep watching the beam from lighthouse shine through the window. It dances across the wall of the room. It quiet me.

I decide to get out. I find a religious man with conscience. He is a minister from small church in village. We make plans.

One afternoon I go for walk. I find dry clothes on washing line. I take shirt and pants and hat. In small alley I change clothes. My uniform I cover with dirt and grass. I keep my head low and walk to ferry. On ferry I sit alone and not talk to no one. When we dock, I walk out with other people.

I had map, and piece of paper from minister for farmer. I not know what the minister wrote. It was in Dutch. I find the farm and hide in barn hayloft. When the farmer come I drop the paper through slats in loft floor.

I look through slats. The farmer reads and looks up. He climb the ladder and look at me without speaking for long time. He go away. Later he come back with blankets, bread, and cheese. "What am I going do with you?" he ask.

The Underground question me. Police question me. I don't know why they not kill me. They move me from farm to attics, cellars, and empty houses. Always questions. Soon they see a poster for reward to catch me. Then they believe. They hear of manhunt on the island and in port. I grow beard and moustache. I worry about my friend on island.

They bring me to your hut. My eyes were cover for the secret trip through forest. If I am caught I will be shot. I not know where they take me now. They want my help with more secrets.

You are brave boy. I would honor a son like you. On outside you are quiet. I see inside too, where you are fearful. I do not know how I can change that. I apologize for my country that makes you afraid.

One day we may meet again. It is hard to be hate by both sides in this war. Maybe you can think kindly of me in your heart.

Your freund *(friend),*
Alfred

CHAPTER EIGHTEEN
HEROES

After Alfred left, nobody came to claim his bunk for a long time. Over the next few months, different people drifted in and out of our hut for a few days, then they'd disappear—to other secret places. I didn't make much of an effort to get to know them because I knew that as soon as I got to know and like people, they would leave. And I was still missing Alfred. Eventually we heard that Alfred returned the next fall, but to a different quadrant. He'd been injured and needed a place to recuperate. We never saw him again.

I shared Alfred's letter with my father and it led us to talk about other acts of bravery. In fact, one was a story we actually experienced—about two brave brothers.

The young men appeared one day in a village. Nobody knew them, so, of course, there were suspicions. Some people thought they were refugees because at that time there were many people on the roads leaving their bombed villages and looking for shelter.

The brothers rode their bicycles everywhere. Their baskets were always full and covered with cloth. Saddlebags on the side seemed to be stuffed. Little did people know that these two were couriers for the Underground. They had first aid supplies in their baskets and food in the saddlebags, along with radios for communication. Their bicycles could arrive at a crash site before the German jeeps because they could cycle through forests and cross fields, where jeeps couldn't go. They'd rescue pilots who had parachuted from burning airplanes.

Then one of the brothers was captured and taken to Westerbork, a work camp. The other brother was outraged and wanted to storm the camp to rescue him. The Underground tried to calm him down, but he insisted. Handing over his papers, just in case he was captured, he left on his bicycle dressed in farmer's clothing. It was almost one hundred kilometers to the camp.

On his way the brother met a Nazi soldier on a motorbike. The soldier stopped the brother and, thinking he was a local, began to question him. When the brother didn't answer, the soldier attacked him. Somehow the brother got hold of the soldier's pistol and shot him. He changed into the Nazi uniform, dressed the dead soldier in the farmer's clothes, hid him, and took the motorbike toward Westerbork.

The brother could speak German so when he got to the camp, he bluffed his way into the commandant's office and said he was there to question the new prisoner. Once he saw that his brother was safe, he told the other personnel that he was transferring him to an interrogation building. He put his brother on the back of the motorbike and raced out of the camp before anyone knew what was happening.

The brothers dodged bullets and jeeps that took up the chase. Roaring through the forest, up hills, and around streams they finally arrived at a "safe" farm where they hid for two days. Then they arrived in our hut. They were spirited away by the Underground after two more days, but those were exciting times as they told their story over and over again.

When I think of them now, I realize just how young they were at the time. One was no more than twenty and the other was high-school age, but more fierce and strong people I've never met.

CHAPTER NINETEEN
PERPETUAL STATE OF WAITING

In the middle of March, 1944, the snow finally ended. For three days it had snowed so much that nobody was able to deliver food. I was looking forward to the visit on Sunday of our former neighbors because they always brought candy for me. I hoped some of the snow would melt. It had been too deep the previous Sunday for our friends to cycle into the woods.

Kazimir had taken me out into the forest to find good wood so he could teach me to carve. He had become friendlier over the months and talked more to us in the evenings. We finally knew his story. It was nothing like I'd imagined. I'll try to repeat what he told us one night while the snow was whirling around.

The trees were like giants swaying in the wind. It was a good night for storytelling with the sound of the wind whistling around the hut.

Kazimir had learned to speak better Dutch since living with us, so it was easier for him to tell his story. He still hesitated while he thought of words and looked to Mama for help. We had to sit close so we could hear his tale.

Kazimir began by saying, "I was a farmer from Siberia and I drove truck for the Russian army when war was declared. I left my family behind and have no word about them."

"Do you have children?" Mama asked.

"Yes, I have one boy and one girl in school. They are with my wife in our town. They must be worried about me. I worry about them," he said.

"How were you captured?" asked the dental student.

"In 1941, Germany attacked Russia. Many of us ran into the forest. But the Nazis ran faster, and most of us were captured."

"How did you end up in Holland?" I asked.

"After I was captured, I was sent to a prison camp in Germany and then transferred to a Dutch camp that needed strong workers. The conditions were so poor that many of the prisoners starved to death. Some were executed when they could not continue working."

He patted his ample stomach. "Luckily I had enough fat so I would not starve," he said, and laughed quietly. I smiled but I wasn't sure if it was all right to laugh with him when he made fun of himself.

Kazimir continued, "One day a truck carrying prisoners was taken into a wooded area. They were to be shot. Before the truck left camp,

I crawled underneath. I hung on to the axle. Once the truck stopped and the prisoners were being unloaded, I crawled out from under the truck and ran, crouching low, into some nearby bushes. I didn't stop to watch the shootings, I just ran and ran."

"And then what happened?" I asked. His story left me breathless.

"I came across a small village, but didn't know much of the language. I just kept asking 'England? England?' I didn't know where I was but I knew where I wanted to go. It was lucky that a soldier didn't see me first. Someone took me to a shopkeeper who knew Russian, and I told him my story. We decided that since I didn't know Dutch, I'd pretend to be his deaf and mute refugee renter. That way nobody would ask questions."

"That's pretty smart," I said.

Kazimir laughed. "I listened and learned as much as I could before I had to leave again. Sometimes I would help in the shop filling shelves, sweeping the floor, and dusting. It was difficult not to speak and to pretend that I wasn't listening."

"And now you're hiding with us. Are you ever going to go and fight again, for Holland?" I asked.

"Walter," Mama said, "that's rude! Why are you asking that?"

"Well, if I were a soldier, I'd want to kill all the Nazis!" I cried out. I was young but I wanted to have a gun so I could shoot the invaders that were in our country. I was angry at how my friends, my family, and I had been treated.

Kazimir just smiled and nodded. "I'm just waiting for the right time and then I'll fight again," he said. "I want to defeat this evil just as much as you do. Every time someone from the Underground comes to visit I ask when I can be of help. They say they'll tell me when they need me."

"Well," said Mama, "in the meantime, I like all the trinkets you're making for us. You can stay with us as long as you like!" Her eyes were brimming with tears. Kazimir held her hand to his face and kissed it.

I had a small wooden boar that Kazimir carved for me. I kept it in my pocket and when I got nervous I rubbed it. Since I got nervous quite often, it became glossy and dark. The smooth surface had a calming effect on me. I kept it until the end of the war, when I felt safe again.

The carvings I made were rough compared to what Kazimir did. Sometimes I got slivers from holding too tightly. When the snow melted I looked for heavier and larger pieces of wood to carve.

Because we were in such close quarters, there were sometimes quarrels. When that happened, I climbed up my ladder and covered myself with blankets. Papa said some people in our little village still didn't trust him because of his German accent. I couldn't hear it anymore. I just heard the Dutch in his and Mama's voices. The older couple and the dental student and his fiancée were from cities, so they weren't used to rough living in a forest. When they wanted to go for walks in the forest for some privacy, Papa said no because it wasn't safe. They had to stay close and they resented Papa telling them what to do. Even Kazimir and I had to stay where we could see the huts.

Our days were so short then, and I felt like I was living in a dark, damp cave. I missed the sunshine. I slept longer because we didn't have enough food to eat. Sleeping kept my mind off the hunger. My stomach grumbled constantly, and my head ached until I ate. I saved the candies until I got so hungry that I thought I'd faint. I hid them so others wouldn't know I had them. I'd go up onto my bed and slowly suck on the sugary goodness until my stomach stopped gurgling for a while.

We all lost weight. I noticed it in the waist of my pants. I had to use rope to hold them up. Living my life in a perpetual state of waiting made me sad and lonely. Sometimes there were days when there were no thoughts in my head at all, and I felt like an empty shell. To keep me busy, Mama put me to work bringing in snow to heat on the stove so we'd have water. The snow was too deep to walk to the new pump, but we had ample amounts of snow to melt for the rest of the winter. Oh, how I longed for spring.

CHAPTER TWENTY
LETTER TO MR. VON BAUMHAUER

17 July, 1944

Dear Mr. von Baumhauer,

I'm hoping to give you this letter when you come to visit tomorrow. I've heard of all the help you've given to build this village and to feed and clothe us and keep us warm. I'm only twelve years old but I know how much of a sacrifice this has been for you. Papa says you've spent a lot of your own money to help us and to hide other Jews. There's a story of how you bribed the Nazis for materials and bicycles for our friends who ride through the forest to bring us food. You spent an entire evening stealing coal from a train boxcar on a sidetrack in a nearby village. Papa says you and your helpers carried coal from the boxcar to trucks and wagons quietly and quickly so you weren't discovered. Because of you, people were warm.

You and my papa are similar. People think my papa is German because of his accent and people may think you're German because of your name. I don't know if you remember me, but we worked side by side when our hidden village was being built. You were very strong and I remember when you brought store-bought lumber for some of the huts.

Before the huts were built, I went to your house with Papa. The first

Although some people were untrustworthy, many others risked their lives to help Jews and other refugees survive the war. Mr. and Mrs. von Baumhauer, whose house is pictured here in 1917, gave generously of their time and money, earning Walter's everlasting gratitude.

time I met you and your wife your voice was gruff, and at first I was scared. But then you smiled and patted me on the shoulder as if to say I was a little man now. I felt appreciated and have always liked you for that.

Your house was beautiful, and I'd sit on the soft leather couch and watch the birds through the large windows. I remember feeling like I was in the forest, even though I was inside. The trees through the windows seemed to reach in and grab me. Your wife brought me cookies and a big glass of milk. My feet couldn't touch the floor so I sat on a pillow on the wood floor and ate my snack from the heavy oak coffee table. The lamps gave off a glow that made me sleepy, and I think I fell asleep on one of our visits.

I just want to thank you and your wife for helping us, and for helping to hide other Jews from the Nazis. I want you to know that we love you and appreciate your sacrifices. I don't know where we'd be now if it weren't for you.

Papa says you do all this because it's the right thing to do. You want to battle the evil that has consumed our country. I hope that when this war is over Holland will give you a big medal. Enclosed in this letter is a medal I made for you from wood. It's round and smooth and I carved a star on it.

Gratefully yours,
Walter

CHAPTER TWENTY-ONE
OPA BAKKER AND TANTE COR

Jenny, my dear granddaughter, you need to know about the people who helped to save your family. We survived because of the people in the Underground and the surrounding villages. Mr. and Mrs. von Baumhauer, and in particular, Opa Bakker and Tante Cor were our heroes. They risked their lives to hide and feed us. I wanted to write a letter to Opa and Tante as well, but they came to visit every Sunday, so I could thank them personally. Mr. von Baumhauer lived in Vierhouten and we occasionally saw him after the village was built.

Every Sunday the people in our hut would clean up and try to prepare a nice table for the visit. Opa and Tante tried to visit each of the nine huts, so we didn't get as much time with them as we wanted. They always brought all the food they could carry and candies for me. In the summer, Mama would serve berries to them. The Bakkers brought cheese and honey from bee farmers. Sometimes there'd be sugarless cakes, and, if we were really lucky, there'd be buns made from grains in the fields. I missed ice cream and whipped cream whenever we ate the berries because that's what I remembered from my youth. My youth—I was still in my youth, but I felt a lot older.

Opa Bakker would tell us stories about the outside world. Sometimes he'd bring us news of the people from Nunspeet—who got married, who had babies, who disappeared. I asked him about Henk and his family and learned that they were fine, living as best they could under the circumstances. Tante Cor told me that Henk asked her if she knew where we'd gone, so I knew he was worried. Of course, she couldn't tell him. We were so close, yet so far from each other. Some days I felt like yelling for Henk from the forest so he'd hear my voice, but that was too dangerous, of course.

One Sunday, Tante Cor told me that Henk's parents were hiding a family in their barn until an attic or cellar could be found somewhere else. I thought about living in that loft where I used to gather the hay. I thought about the lowing of the cows that might soothe the frightened family hiding in dark corners, covered with hay. I had pleasant memories of that barn, but I'd been there when I was free. I don't know what I'd have felt if that hayloft had been my hiding place.

One Sunday I made a card for Opa Bakker and Tante Cor and gave it to them. It said "Thank You" in large letters with a flower on the cover. Inside I drew some lips to show a kiss and a big circle for a hug. Tante Cor gave me a hug when she read it. It was like being hugged by my oma, and it made me miss her even more.

For their bravery and human kindness, Opa Bakker and Tante Cor are honored on the plaque at the Hidden Village site. At great risk to their own safety they steadfastly brought food, news of the war, and hope to the onderduikers.

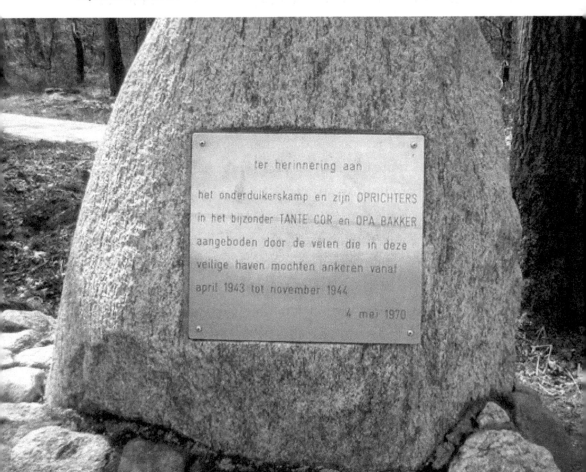

CHAPTER TWENTY-TWO
ATTACK!

4 November, 1944

Dear Oma,

We were attacked six days ago! We're safe, so don't worry. I'm just now able to think about the events without shaking. Last night was the first time I slept without having nightmares. Since starting to write these letters, I've discovered how healing they can be, so I'm going to relive the experience as much for my sake as yours. I'm treating it as a writing assignment for school. How's that for turning terror into homework?

It began with a shout. I was standing near the hut, just as dusk turned into night, trying to decide where I should pick mushrooms. It was so quiet. Suddenly I heard "Heraus! Uit!" (Out!) in both languages. For a split second I was frozen, and then I ran.

My lungs filled with air as I gasped in fear and fled forward into the surrounding forest. I didn't know where Mama and Papa were, but Papa had told me to just run if we were attacked—"Do whatever it takes to survive."

My heart felt like it was in my throat. I couldn't swallow. My lungs burned and the air I tried to breathe didn't seem to reach them. With my hands flung in front of me to avoid hitting trees, I spun away and into the dark. In my haste, I fell. My knees hit the dirt, but I was up in an instant, even though I felt the mud sliding beneath my boots.

My breathing was loud and raspy, and I was losing my breath. I opened my mouth to take in great gobs of air, and I ran faster than I'd ever run before. Still, it felt like everything was happening in slow motion.

Shots rang out behind me, and snapping branches sounded ahead of me. People running for their lives, or Nazis smashing through the forest? When I looked over my shoulder, the streaks of light from the attackers' guns told me that they'd surrounded the village. They'd actually come into the forest to kill us. So much for not getting their boots dirty!

Explosions and flashes lit up the darkness behind, illuminating fleeing figures and spaces between the trees. I don't know how I noticed all this while running for my life, but everything seemed to happen slowly, and the thoughts and images flitted through my mind unhampered. I felt branches scraping my face and arms, smelled the cold earth, and felt the wetness of the air. My breathing was heavier now but more even.

Unexpectedly, I tripped and nosedived into the cold earth. I crawled across the dirt and stood up again. My toe hurt, but I had to keep going.

Between the rapid shots, rushing feet surrounded me, and I ran even faster. Sweat trickled down my face and stung my eyes.

Up ahead, a heavy shadow was crouched low to the ground. A neighbor stopping to rest, or a Nazi taking aim? With a surge of speed, I ran past and stepped on something fleshy. A scream, then a German curse. I zigged and zagged, crouching close to the ground through the trees, expecting bullets to follow. A yell of pain rang out, and gunfire sounded over my head as I darted sideways through the forest.

Fear had overtaken my body. My only thought was survive. *As I ran, the gunshots became fewer and fewer, and were replaced with loud guttural shouts, engines revving, and vehicles racing along the fire roads. The Nazis were trying to surround us.*

I had to stop to catch my breath. My chest heaved. I bent down with my hands on my knees, inhaling and exhaling slowly and deeply. My head hurt, my toe throbbed, my face felt hot. Both eyes burned from the sweat running down my forehead, and I realized I'd also wet myself from fear. I bent down and grabbed some of the cool earth in my hand and smeared it on my face and neck to cool off.

I got down onto my stomach and crawled over roots and branches on the ground, clawing my way forward with my fingers. My senses were on alert for any sound or movement.

I heard an explosion, and the faint smell of smoke wafted on the breeze. I looked behind me and saw a light glow in the distance. My village was on fire! My stomach climbed into my throat and my eyes filled. With clenched fists I wiped away the tears. I had to stop myself from crying by biting my lip so hard that pain replaced anger.

It was quiet ahead of me. I raised myself to my knees, then to my feet and walked, bent over, to the edge of the forest. I saw no people or vehicles. The closer I got, the clearer the road seemed to be. The attack sounds were getting fainter and fainter.

As I stepped into a clearing I recognized where I was. If I followed the fire path along in the direction away from the village, I knew I would get

Dense forest on either side of the fire roads made the camouflaged dwellings nearly impossible for Nazi patrols to see. Noise was far more likely to betray the fugitives, especially after the forest workers had left for the day

to a neighboring town. There would be farms with barns and haylofts. I crept along the edge of the forest, ready to dash in at any sound. My heart was beating quickly, but my head was clear, and I was planning my escape.

Figures appeared ahead of me and just as I was set to run, I heard a loud whisper.

"Walter!"

"Papa?"

Mama and Papa were huddled under a tree. I ran to them as silently as I could, threw myself into Papa's arms, and cried quietly. His hands patted my back and Mama encircled us with her arms.

Mama and Papa, like me, were dirty and wet. Soil clung to their hair and fingers. Dirty smudges covered their faces. I saw scratches on Mama's arms. She was shivering in her dress, and Papa kept his arm around her. In the shock and surprise of the attack there'd been no time to grab rucksacks or sweaters; we'd escaped with just the clothes on our backs.

Silently we started moving, always watching and listening. It seemed like a long time before a large barn loomed directly in front of us. We inched forward and found the main door that was slightly open. Once inside, I saw a ladder that would take us up to the hayloft. Some of the cows mooed quietly, annoyed that we had awakened them.

Papa didn't need to tell me what to do. I crawled across the hay until I found a place where I could cover myself. I didn't dare talk. That would have to wait until Papa determined it was safe. I just burrowed down into the hay and, despite wanting to stay alert, I fell asleep. That barn was our home for the next two nights. And then we ended up here.

I'll write more later, but first I have some sad news. In my hurry to run, Affe was left behind. That sock monkey has always been with me since you made him, Oma. I feel so badly about abandoning him, but there was no choice. Maybe he survived the attack and one day another little boy will find him in the forest.

Your tired but grateful to be alive grandson,
Walter

CHAPTER TWENTY-THREE
AFTERMATH

Jenny, reading that old letter about the attack brought back all the fear I experienced that day, but I'll try to describe what happened after that.

When I awoke the morning after our escape, I heard the farmer in the barn below. He was sweeping the hay, and the dust floated up into our loft, making the air hazy. I hoped I wouldn't cough. The cows, lowing quietly, seemed content. I must have missed the milking while I was asleep. I'd always liked the sound of the milk pinging against the metal pails and the rich warm smell.

I didn't dare look up to see Papa or Mama. I lay on my stomach and watched the farmer below through a crack in the floor, not moving lest I made a sound. It was cold and I was hungry. After a while the warmth from the cows below and the hay in the loft put me to sleep again. I'd put a handkerchief around my mouth the night before to prevent myself from calling out in case I had nightmares. I was still wearing it.

I slept off and on during the day, dreaming about the shooting, the shouting, the forest. It felt like I was running again and I woke up once to my feet stirring up the hay. I looked through the crack in the floor to make sure the farmer hadn't heard me. He wasn't there. Breathing a sigh of relief, I wished for darkness so I could take off my gag, stretch my muscles, and whisper to my family.

Once the farmer left for the night, Papa slipped out. I heard him rustling around in the hay. I looked up, and in the moonlight coming through the gaps in the barn boards, I saw him put his fingers to his lips, then point to where Mama was sitting. He climbed down the ladder and I wouldn't see him again until morning.

Mama beckoned me over. She spoke in a whisper so low that I had to bend closer to hear. "Your father is going to find help."

"Whose farm is this? Do you know the farmer?" I whispered back.

Mama shook her head no. "I think it might be a 'safe' barn."

I shrugged my shoulders and held out my hands as if to ask "Why?"

"Some farmers leave their barn doors open in case people need refuge. They don't want to know who's hiding or why. That way if the Nazis come looking, the farmer won't have to lie. We're hoping that this farmer is one of the friendly ones."

"Where's Papa going?" I asked in a low whisper.

Mama held her arm tightly around my shoulders. "He's going to find a local resident who's connected to the Underground. I'm sure everyone knows what's happened by now. The Underground will need to find the rest of the villagers and move them to safer places."

"Will we ever see anyone from the village again?" I asked.

"I don't know. They may have scattered to the winds."

"How did you and Papa stay together when you were running?" I asked.

"Your father grabbed my hand and just pulled me along," she said. "At one point when I got so winded, he lifted me up over his shoulders. The trees scratched both of us, but we just kept running.

"I'm sorry, Walter. The attack was so sudden I forgot all about grabbing rucksacks, so we have no clothing." She shook her head and covered her face with her hands.

"We're alive and that's all that counts," I said, and put my arm around her for comfort. "We've lived in the same clothing for days at other times, so it's nothing new."

I settled down in the hay to sleep while Mama kept watch. I offered to stay up, but she said I should sleep. I put the handkerchief across my mouth and closed my eyes. The next thing I felt was a touch on my shoulder. Papa was smiling down at me.

"Time to eat," he said.

The early morning light filtered through the cracks in the walls and cast beams of light on the hay. Papa's walking and talking normally meant we were alone. I wondered why the farmer wasn't in the barn, because cows are usually milked early in the morning, sometimes even before the sun comes up. I sat up in the hay. My muscles felt stiff, and I stretched high and sideways to get out the kinks.

Papa had sausages and bread. He handed the food to Mama and me. We attacked that meal like ravenous dogs. I wrapped the bread around the sausage and crammed it into my mouth. Chewing so much food hurt my jaw, and swallowing had to be done in stages. I felt like a squirrel with cheeks puffed out, full of food.

Mama put her hand on my shoulder. "Walter, Walter, slow down or you'll choke."

Papa had a small bottle of wine that he passed around. As I was gorging myself, I gave Papa a questioning look.

He understood my raised eyebrows. "I went to a man who helped us build our hidden village. He shared some of his food. He's a very generous man and he contacted the Underground. People will be coming for us soon with bicycles."

As brighter sunlight started to seep through the loft slats, I got worried again. What if the farmer came into the barn and heard us? "Where is he? Why isn't he in the barn milking his cows?" I asked.

"The farmer and his family decided to sleep late this morning," said Papa and he winked and smiled. "Soon we'll hear a signal to leave. Finish your food and drink so we'll be ready."

In a few minutes, a bird-like whistle wafted up into the loft. Papa rose and beckoned for us to follow him. We climbed down the ladder and walked out into the barnyard. Two men on bicycles handed us jackets and scarves for warmth.

One of the men was the person Papa contacted. He helped me into a buckboard that was attached to the front of his bicycle, and Papa hopped on the seat at the back. We were a heavy load for that cyclist. The second man put my mother into a wagon behind his bicycle. He gave her a covered basket and a kerchief for her head.

There were tools in the buckboard, and it looked as if we were on our way to work. Our destination, said one of the men, was a village about forty kilometers away from the farm.

"With all the refugees, you'll fit in nicely," said one of the men. "There's a farmhouse where you can stay with a family. They think you're from Arnhem, so if you've never been there, you might want to keep more to yourselves to avoid any questions."

One of the men handed some papers to Papa. "Here are your new identities," he said.

Papa gave me my papers and said, "Welcome, Henk de Jong from Arnhem. How do you do? I am Erwin de Jong, and this is your mama, Loes de Jong." We shook hands across the bicycles and smiled broadly. It was easy to remember my first name because of my friend Henk, but I had to repeat my new last name over and over. Our birthdays were the same, so we could remember them. So that part was easier.

Off we went, the bicycle wheels bumping over the rough roads. Along the way, as the morning progressed, we passed other people on bikes, front baskets loaded with bags. Some walked, carrying suitcases, and others carried their possessions in their arms or over their shoulders.

"Many of these people are refugees who've been evicted from their homes in and around Arnhem. Some of the homes were destroyed in a battle between the Allies and the Nazis last month. There was extensive bombing, and many people were killed. Anyone who survived had to leave." The man pedaling my bike told me this when he saw me turning from side to side to look at the people.

"But where will they all go?" I asked. "What about the homes that are still standing? Who's living there?" I tried to turn around to face the cyclist so I could hear him better.

"Their homes have been looted, we just discovered, and their possessions sent to Germany. So they, like you, are homeless," he said. *Homeless*—the word burrowed deep into my brain.

I felt sorry for those people because I knew how it felt to leave home. Who was living in my room? Where was the cat? I worried about Den Haag because we'd heard about the terrible bombing of the cities. What about my father's store and the man who was looking after it? Would they be there when we got back? If we got back.

I was anxious to know the details of the attack on our Hidden Village. How did the Nazis find us? What happened to the other villagers? Was everything destroyed? I knew Papa would tell me when he found out. I was afraid to hear about it in case someone from our hut had died.

In the box where I was riding, there was a burlap bag tied at its top. I twisted around, pointed at the sack and gave the cyclist a look that asked if I could peek inside. He nodded yes. I untied the knot and found sweaters, jackets, and other thick pieces of clothing I couldn't make out. I pulled out a large sweater and pulled it over the jacket I was wearing because I was getting cold.

I wondered if the basket my mother was holding was also filled with extra clothing. It was amazing how the Underground worked to make sure everyone was safe. We owed them so much for putting their lives at risk to keep us out of danger. I closed my eyes and prayed the war would end soon.

Finally, we got to the edge of a town. An unpainted sign said Ermelo. Our cyclists dismounted, and we got off the bikes. One man gave Papa a map with directions to where we were going. I had to get used to being called Henk now.

"Speak as little as possible because you still have a tiny trace of a German accent," the man said. "Stay away from other refugees in case they begin to talk about Arnhem."

"This particular farmer isn't happy about having to share his family home and food. He made sure to tell us that if we sent him Jews to hide, he'd report them and us. Farms have been burned to the ground and farmers killed if they were found to be hiding Jews. This farmer isn't a bad man. He's just protecting his family. You have to be very cautious now," the other cyclist added.

One of the men put his hand on Papa's shoulder. "The Allies are beginning to make headway, and everyone hopes the war will soon be over, but we're not out of the woods yet."

Papa and I heard his play on words and laughed. "Well, we are out of the woods at least."

The man gave Papa a folded piece of paper, jumped on his bicycle, and both men rode off. On the paper were names of trusted contacts in the town. We set off to meet our new hosts.

CHAPTER TWENTY-FOUR
THE WHISPERING STOPS

10 November, 1944

Dear Oma,

I'm reflecting on the past twenty-one months. Since leaving our summer home, I've learned to whisper at all times, lived in a caravan, been enclosed in a forest, built a village, lived with strangers, had two narrow escapes from the Nazis, and experienced constant fear.

Now I no longer have to whisper, and the sunshine feels warm on my skin. It's a feeling I had forgotten. I still have to squint to see and put my hand up to shield my eyes. The days are getting colder, and the trees have lost their leaves, but the sun shines as if no problems exist.

A man from the Underground showed us the way to this farm when we arrived here. As I walked along carrying our new belongings, the sack slung over my shoulder, I kept repeating my new name over and over again.

When we arrived, I saw a white wooden house with a verandah across the front. It stretched back a long way and there were black-framed windows in the walls. The farmer came out from the barn to greet us as we entered the yard. He showed us the entrance to the house and the backyard that bordered a forested area. He called his wife to let us in.

I stayed behind to look at the surroundings. There was a large unpainted barn and two or three smaller sheds, also made of rough wood. I wondered if I'd be able to help the farmer with his chores. As I was thinking that, a young man walked out of the barn, came over to us and greeted the farmer as "Papa." He smiled at us and held out his hand to be shaken. The farmer grumbled something and took us into the house.

We were shown to a tiny room in the back. It's furnished with one bed and a small couch without arms. There is a low chest of drawers along one wall and hooks on the back of the door for the little clothing we have. A tiny window looks out onto the backyard and into the forested area. Under the window is a small table and one chair. My bed is the couch. The couch is so short that my feet hang over the side, so I put the chair at the end when I sleep.

We have to share the bathroom with our host family, and the wife showed us how to clean it after every use. It's almost as if she doesn't want strangers sitting on her toilet. That makes me smile, but it also makes me worry. What if I forget? The bathtub hangs on a wall in the outside shed. The family brings it into the kitchen every Saturday and we'll take turns using it for bathing. We have our baths after the family.

The wife showed us the "Sunday room," which is used only on Sundays and is kept clean and tidy. There's a harmonium against one wall. It looks like our piano with the keyboard but has wider pedals and sounds a bit like an accordion. Mama's eyes lit up when she first saw it. She walked over to it, and her hands brushed over the keyboard. The wife noticed and asked, "Do you play?"

Mama nodded. The wife pulled out the seat and offered Mama the chance to play. The music filled the room and gave me goose bumps. After the piece was finished, the wife and her son, who'd come in from outside, clapped. Mama bowed her head and nodded to the wife with a smile. Neither Mama nor Papa had spoken yet, and neither had I. So far, I thought, so good.

After that, we went back to our room, emptied the sack and basket of clothing and hung the clothes on the hooks. We sat and waited until it was time for supper—Mama on the bed, Papa on the couch, and I on the chair. Each of us was lost in our own thoughts and looking out the window.

Finally we were called for supper. That was the first time in many months that we ate a normal supper in a normal kitchen with normal plates and windows that looked out onto freedom.

That first night at supper we had potatoes and sausage. After eating so little meat over the last year and a half, to have sausage twice in a few days made my stomach happy.

"This sausage is from the last calf on this farm. I have no more cows to slaughter," the farmer said.

We all looked down at our plates.

"Meat will be rare or unavailable in the coming months," he continued in a gruff voice.

We nodded but I felt myself getting hot.

"I have some dairy cows for milk and cheese but they're not producing very much anymore. So don't expect much from our cupboards." I felt like a child again being scolded by a strict teacher.

After supper we went for a walk in the forest behind the house. When we returned, the son, who's about eighteen years old, tried to have a conversation with me. I pretended I was shy, which wasn't far from the truth. I wasn't sure how to answer his questions, so I said, "I don't know." His mother said he should leave us alone because we were probably still upset from having to leave our home. That was a good excuse for us not to talk.

Afterward in our room, we talked in whispers. We're used to this. Along with the sunshine, being able to talk out loud is going to be a treat for me. In our room we always whisper for privacy and to make sure nobody can hear Mama and Papa's accents.

We are finally free and safe—or are we? We still can't relax and let our guard down. We can't use our own names. We can't speak much, although I have a good Dutch accent. Mama and Papa's German accents are fading more and more each day, but we still think it best if they don't speak much to the farmer and his family.

I've told the family that we don't want to talk about our experiences because they've been too horrible. They nodded, but the farmer stood by with his arms folded, looking at us as if he didn't believe us. I felt beads of perspiration begin on my forehead.

I talked to Papa about helping the farmer with his chores because I enjoyed helping where we lived before. And maybe the farmer would trust us more.

"The more we stay out of his way, the better it'll be for everyone," Papa said.

So, here I am, spending my time writing letters to tell you about our terrifying adventures. And now that they're over, you don't need to worry because we're safe.

When the man from the Underground comes to see how we are, I'll give him this letter. I think it might get harder and harder for you to receive my letters because I think there are more important issues facing the Underground, like trying to win this war.

Your growing grandson,
Walter

CHAPTER TWENTY-FIVE
MAKING THE BEST OF A BAD SITUATION

On one of our daily walks into the forest behind the farm I asked Papa about the people we'd seen walking and riding along the roads, some slowly shuffling along in torn shoes, carrying sacks, and pulling wagons with small children. I remember our conversation at the time.

"We aren't the only people without a home," I said. "I wonder every night if the Underground has found other farmers who share their shelter and food. With the farm families living on bare supplies, how can they feed more?"

"Many Dutch people have left the cities, because they've been devastated by bombs. There is no food so people flee to the countryside. There are still some farms that grow crops and raise a few animals. But feed for the animals is also becoming scarce."

"How will the people get food? Where will they stay?"

"These people are bringing their valuables to trade for food. Our farmer has probably traded a lot of his meat and vegetables with refugees who came looking for something to eat. So now his family is also low on supplies, although they have a lot of potatoes in the shed."

"I can eat potatoes every day, even if they don't have butter." I smiled.

"How has it gotten to be so bad that even here there isn't any food?" Mama asked.

"The Nazis flooded farmland this past summer, so many crops were ruined," Papa said. "This just added to the scarcity of food. When the Dutch railroad workers went on strike in September, no food could get into the cities or towns by rail. So the Nazis banned all other food transportation in Holland."

"Is that why everyone is coming here by bicycle and on foot?" my mother asked.

"Yes."

"Why is there a railroad strike?" I asked.

"The exiled Dutch government thought if there was a rail strike, the Nazis wouldn't be able to move their troops or equipment. The Allies would have a better chance of defeating them. But it seems that since September, the Nazis have been using their own trains. They threatened that a strike would endanger the food supply and that has happened—they have retaliated."

"This is going to be a long hard winter," Mama said.

Over the next few weeks, as late autumn turned to winter, Papa and I would leave the farmhouse every day and walk into town. We'd look in store windows and avoid making eye contact with anyone. Sometimes, we'd go to the village to buy bread, find a bench, and share the bread with each other.

We didn't have much money left from what the butcher had sent so long ago. Bread was expensive. The money from my father's shop hadn't been getting to us since we'd gone into hiding, and we had only the remainder of what we'd taken when we left the summer house, twenty-one months earlier. Papa used some of that to buy us new rucksacks to use when we had to move again. The burlap bag was too cumbersome to carry, especially if we had to run.

Families had to use coupons or ration stamps for food. Each person was allowed only five slices of bread, three small potatoes, five grams of cheese, and twenty-eight grams of peas per week. It wasn't enough for a family to live on, and when a second family lived in the same house, it was even less.

To avoid getting in the way of the family, and when it got too cold to walk to town, we'd walk in the woods behind the house, where we felt more comfortable, sheltered by trees once again.

CHAPTER TWENTY-SIX
LEARNING ABOUT THE ATTACK

Papa finally told us about the attack on the Hidden Village.

One cold day in early December, Papa said he had something important to tell us. Mama carried out a blanket to put on a fallen log behind the farm and we sat together. It hadn't snowed much yet, but the air carried a hint of what was to come. We were wearing winter sweaters under jackets.

Mama seemed to know what Papa was going to tell us. I guess after twenty years of marriage, couples can read each other's thoughts and expressions.

"How did the Nazis find us?"

"Nobody knows, but the Underground thinks the attackers were SS. There are rumors, but in all the chaos there's no confirming how they discovered us. There were no witnesses because everybody ran.

Villagers from Vierhouten saw the SS and soldiers returning after the attack." Papa shook his head at the memory.

"Did everyone escape?" I asked in a shaky voice.

Papa took a deep breath. "A husband and his sick wife stopped to rest near the village after the attack and were captured. The woman died in the night and her husband was killed the next day.

"Six people were taken prisoner. A father and his six-year-old son were captured as they tried to escape. A family of three—a father, mother, and adult son—tried to hide in their hut but were found. The wife was ill and her husband and son wouldn't leave her. Alfred carried out an old man over his shoulders. They were caught and the old man was shot with the other five villagers two days later, on October 31. Because Alfred was a deserter he had to be taken back to his unit where he'd be executed, but we heard that he escaped. We don't know where he is now. But he was heroic to risk his life to save someone else."

We sat there in shock. It was scary to hear about their deaths, knowing how close I'd come to being shot. I felt sad for the young boy and his father, and for the other families.

"I hope all the others escaped with their lives. How many people escaped? What about our little village? Is it totally destroyed?" asked Mama.

Papa nodded and told us that after the shooting stopped, the soldiers went in with grenades and blew up all the huts. There had been almost a hundred people in the village at the time, and now the survivors had all disappeared.

I shuddered to think that when we were in the barn, we could have been discovered. We were so close to the forest and perhaps the caravan of trucks passed by our hiding place.

"Where are all the villagers now?" I asked.

"Only the Underground knows," Papa said. "Everyone scattered and ended up in different places. They hid until they could be rescued or join other refugees coming from the cities. We'll probably never see anyone from our quadrant or the village again. With all the refugees, hiding places are becoming more scarce, so we're lucky to be at this farm."

The names of the eight "Villagers" who died in the raid on the Hidden Village are engraved on this memorial. The people who escaped scattered and their whereabouts remained largely unknown.

"At least we're still together, not like others who might be wandering alone and lost somewhere," Mama said, as she gazed out into the forest. She shook her head, heaved a sigh, got up, and folded the blanket. It was our signal to go back to our reality.

That night I went to bed hungry and cried myself to sleep. People were predicting a bad winter. Food was scarce, people were displaced, and the war was still raging in our country. What kind of life could we expect when we woke up every morning? When would we have a normal life again? When would I see Hannah and Oma? Would the farmer discover we're Jewish? How could we bury our true identities and survive while hiding in plain view?

CHAPTER TWENTY-SEVEN
HIDING IN PLAIN VIEW

10 December, 1944

Dear Oma,

We've been careful not to attract attention to ourselves. Sinterklaas didn't visit this farm five nights ago. He was mentioned, but no gifts were left on the doorstep. But the wife gave me an extra potato for supper. Now something else has happened to scare us.

The farm wife wants Mama to play Christmas songs on their harmonium. Mama panicked because she doesn't know any Christmas songs, only Yiddish songs. Because I learned the songs in school, I've been teaching her the words and the music to O Tannenbaum and Silent Night. Since Mama plays by ear, she's been practicing on the chest of drawers in our room, pretending it's the keyboard.

Now that we have a job—to teach Mama—we have an excuse to leave the house and walk deep into the woods, through the snow. We sit on old downed logs and sing the songs together. It still feels strange to speak much above a whisper after living nearly mute for so long.

A few days ago I asked the farmer's wife if Mama could practice on the harmonium because it had been so long since she'd played. I pretended we'd had a harmonium in our home in Arnhem and I told the wife that we'd sold it for food money. She seemed to believe me and was sympathetic. For the first time I saw her soft side.

For the last few nights Mama has played and the farmer's family has joined us in singing the songs. There are a lot of songs to teach, so when Mama runs out of material she shows that she's tired and goes to bed. She learns more from me the next day and keeps the family's suspicions at bay.

When we walk into town now, the roads are icy and it takes longer. We wear our hats low over our faces so nobody recognizes us. Papa and I look in windows, and I daydream about what I'm going to buy when the war ends. I have to think positively to avoid having nightmares and alerting the family with my screams.

Something strange happened a week ago when we were in the village after the music lessons. Papa saw a woman on a bicycle crunching along the snowy street. He recognized her. Papa dragged me into a store and watched through the window until the woman rode past. She'd looked at Papa and seemed to know him, too. Papa couldn't remember how he knew her.

We left immediately for the farm and walked quickly. We heard tire sounds on the ice and snow behind us. The same woman on the bicycle rode past us with a piece of paper in her hand to give to Papa, but he wouldn't acknowledge her. She dropped the paper and continued riding.

Papa picked up the paper and read: *If you are ever in danger, here's my address.* Slowly Papa smiled when he read the signature.

"This is a friend from Den Haag," Papa said. "She is Italian-Jewish and married to a Dutch man who used to buy his coffee from me."

"Why is she living here now?" I asked.

"Something must have happened to make them leave the city. She's lost so much weight I hardly recognized her."

The next day Papa walked into town to see if he could find the woman. I stayed home and taught Mama more carols. That night he came home with news.

He was excited when he spoke. "The woman returned to pick up supplies. We sat on a bench and talked. Her husband is now a prisoner of war, and she moved from Den Haag to avoid suspicion falling on her and her two daughters. They're living on the outskirts of a nearby town and she said that if we ever needed a place to stay, we could just arrive at her doorstep and she'd welcome us."

Mama's eyes grew wide and she clasped her fingers in front of her chest. Her mouth formed an O, and then she smiled. I think she was hoping to escape playing the Christmas songs.

"It's only six kilometers away, so we can walk if we have to escape quickly," Papa said.

When she heard about another long walk, Mama's head dropped, and her smile disappeared. "When will this all be over?" And she wept.

Papa gathered us both in his arms and told us what he'd heard in town.

"The Allies are making great gains, and the South is almost rid of the Nazis. The Nazis are concentrating their efforts in bigger centers and in areas where there are bridges and rail lines to prevent an attack from the North. Smaller towns like this aren't as important to them right now, so it'll be easier to run without being spotted."

I tried to cheer up Mama. "And we look like all the other refugees, so nobody will be suspicious. I have a good feeling that this war will be over soon, and we can go home again."

Then I started to sing a carol and made Mama laugh. She pushed me on the shoulder and I collapsed on the bed laughing.

That night around the supper table we ate oats cooked in water. Everyone was thinking his or her own thoughts. I was wondering how many more farms and houses we would visit before we could go home. How much warning will we have before we have to run again? Will we be able to stay together? I stirred the oats and thought and stirred and thought. I felt the farmer's wife's hand on mine, and she smiled a sympathetic smile as if she could read my mind.

Even though I'm thirteen, part of me is still a frightened child. The other part wants to fight and drive out the invaders. That night we checked our new rucksacks and made sure they were ready for flight. Papa and I always wear ours to town in case we can't get home. We have a pre-arranged meeting spot in the event we all get separated.

On this note I leave you. Christmas is coming, and our hosts are more cheerful. Mama knows how to play Christmas songs, and Papa and I sing along with the family so they can't hear our mistakes. There's snow on the trees and frost on the windows. For all the beauty surrounding us, there's still fear in my heart.

Walter

CHAPTER TWENTY-EIGHT

ON THE RUN AGAIN

Two days before Christmas, an Underground group was discovered by the Nazis. The leader was only twenty-three. He was among those killed. Others just disappeared. A visitor came to the farmhouse a few days later and gave us the news. He told Papa that they didn't know how much the Nazis had discovered from their prisoners, so it would be best if we left. Papa informed him about the woman's offer of a safe place to hide. I think that was a relief for the man because he wouldn't have to find another place for us. That afternoon Papa, Mama, and I went for a walk to the village with our rucksacks on our backs, and just kept walking. We never said good-bye to the farmer and his family.

As we walked, Mama told us that she was sad that we hadn't thanked our hosts. She knew what a risk it was for them to shelter Jews, even though we had our new identities.

"They'll think we're ungrateful, and I want to tell them how much we appreciated sharing their home and food."

"If the Underground information was compromised, the Nazis will discover our true identities and harm will come, not only to us, but to the farmer as well," Papa said. "It's best that we leave without telling him, so he knows nothing if the Nazis come looking."

"At least now you don't have to play Christmas music," I chirped. Mama smiled and ruffled my hair.

We walked through deep snow and eventually got to the woman's house in the countryside. There was no light coming from her windows, but we knew the family was home. We knocked on a carved wooden door attached with large metal hinges. It was almost dawn. They might have been frightened to hear a knock at that time.

Angela, Papa's friend, cautiously opened the door. She welcomed us inside. We stepped into a large room, illuminated by a coal oil lamp on a table. It was warmer inside, but Angela and two young girls were wearing heavy sweaters over nightshirts.

"These are my daughters, Isabella and Doortje," she said. "They are around your age, Walter, and have wanted a new friend for a long time."

There was a kettle of hot water on the stove, and Angela made hot tea from potato peels. While the taste wasn't so great, the warmth of the water felt good. Isabella and Doortje sat beside me. They smiled and looked me over. I felt my cheeks get hot.

When I entered this house I just knew it was going to be a place of comfort at last. I felt accepted by these new strangers. Every day I felt more of my fear draining. I wondered if I should let myself hope.

The house was small with a thatched roof and whitewashed plaster. The windows were little, like in a fairy tale house. There were two large rooms on the first floor; one was the kitchen and eating area and the other, a sitting area. The kitchen had a large stove and a table with three chairs, all different styles. There was a pile of roughly cut wooden branches beside the stove and a pail with coal. I was surprised to see the coal because it was hard to find.

The sitting area had a fireplace but it wasn't being used because there wasn't enough wood for it. One couch was covered with a thin blanket, and in a corner by a window sat a shiny black piano. My mother walked over to it and ran her fingers along its glossy finish. I could see her eyes light up when she first discovered it. We had music every day because Angela also played. But no Christmas songs!

Our sleeping area was in the sitting space with blankets spread on the couch and floor. Angela and her daughters slept upstairs under the steep attic roof.

Between the eating and sitting areas there was a small room with a toilet, and a tub that stood on four claw legs. What a joy it was for me to see an actual inside toilet and a real bathtub! Every time I used either one, I gave thanks in my head.

To bathe we filled the bathtub with water from melted snow heated in large pots on the stove. It was so cold in that room that we rarely wanted to have a bath. Even if the water was warm, when we stepped out, our skin felt like ice. But, of course, the morning we arrived we all had a bath because of the novelty, and the hot water helped our chilled bones. After my bath I burrowed myself under four blankets on the couch and fell asleep instantly amidst the conversations going on.

I loved our time with this family and didn't want it to ever end. Isabella, Doortje, and I played in the snow outside without fear of being discovered. I still had my new identity tucked away, but I was Walter once again.

Angela's identification showed her Northern Italian side, so if anyone asked who we were, she said we were her husband's relatives escaping the bombing of Arnhem. We didn't look anything like Angela with her blonde hair and blue eyes. Papa and I had brown hair and eyes, and Mama had red hair, hazel eyes, and freckles. So we had to be related to her Dutch husband. That was a good thing because I'd heard he was very brave.

At first, I was afraid to go outside after hiding for so long. Papa encouraged me to venture out. "Soldiers have better things to do than watch children playing," he said. So I let myself relax more.

I could finally speak out loud and even shout. I could use my own name. I could play outside in the sunshine, and roll in the snow with my two new friends. Mama played the piano every day. Papa went into the surrounding woods to cut firewood. It was a happy house, even though we were still in hiding and a long way from home.

CHAPTER TWENTY-NINE
MOMENTARY RESPITE

Angela's farmhouse was on the outskirts of Harderwijk. This is where we lived for fifty glorious days, and I loved it. At the end of the war we discovered that Oma had been hiding inside the town of Harderwijk, just a short distance away. How close we were, and yet how far! I smiled when I realized that the Underground didn't have that far to go to deliver my letters.

My father eventually got a message to a new Underground "cell" to tell them of our whereabouts in case we had to be moved again. Angela knew where to deliver the message and my letters. Because she used her husband's surname, nobody suspected she was half Jewish, so she could move around with ease. The Nazis had banned all radios by this time so Angela's contacts had to be in person. Isabella, Doortje, and I would virtually hold our breaths until we saw her walking or cycling toward us after her trips to the village. The three of us were scared whenever any parent left the house.

Angela had no food stamps, so she would trade some of the old tea she had been hoarding for oats and cheese. She'd already sold some of her possessions for milk for her daughters. This was the winter that became known as *hongerwinter*. People all over Holland were starving and the weather was unusually cold that year.

The Allies were invading and there were fierce battles in many areas. The South had been liberated before Christmas, and we in the North were hoping that we'd be liberated soon. To make matters worse, as the Allies advanced, the Nazis started grabbing men and boys off the streets to work as laborers. We worried that they would begin combing the countryside for available men and boys, so for the last few weeks of our stay, my father and I were once more restricted to the house. Luckily nobody knocked on the door or snooped around.

CHAPTER THIRTY
THE ENCHANTED FARMHOUSE

3 February, 1945

Dear Oma,

I had to write to tell you about an exciting event. We had eggs for the first time in almost two years! But first I have to tell you that we are no longer on the farm. We are staying with a friend of Papa's in the countryside. We have been here since just before Christmas. I like it very much.

Papa's friend (I can't tell you her real name, so I will just call her AC) found someone whose chickens hadn't frozen to death. She traded a jacket Mama made, from one of the old threadbare blankets, for six eggs. We melted snow on the stove and boiled the eggs. I enjoyed my egg by taking tiny bites and rolling it around inside my mouth. I hated to see it disappear.

Our stove burns wood from nearby trees that Papa chops. AC miracu-lously shows up some days with coal in a sack. I always wonder where she got it and what she had to trade. Luckily we have sweaters to keep us warm, so we rationed the coal for when it got extremely cold. AC told us that many people who have no fuel burn their furniture when they run out of trees.

We eat soup made from tulip bulbs and potato peels. The ingredients in one pancake recipe are mashed tulip bulbs, potatoes, and water. We have potatoes because they grew well in AC's garden and keep well in the cold. Sometimes when we have cheese, we melt a little bit onto our potatoes to get a different taste.

There's no electricity, but AC has a generator that she runs with her bicycle, so some nights we have light. We take turns riding the bicycle on a rack, to run the generator. We get our exercise even though we can't cycle very long on empty stomachs. On particularly cold days, we never get out of bed because it's warmer under the blankets. I've noticed that my trousers are getting too big for me and I have to use twine to hold them up.

It's time to go out and play now. The sun is shining, and it's hard to look at the snow. Today we're going to build a snow house. I'm having so much fun here!

I'll write more later.
Walter

CHAPTER THIRTY-ONE
ON THE MOVE AGAIN

Near the middle of February 1945, it became too dangerous for us to stay in Angela's house because the Nazis were widening their searches for laborers. All their workers had gone to the front lines, so they needed local men. The Underground came with bicycles with wide wooden wheels that worked in the snow. The stones on the roads were peeking out of the snow and it was easier to cycle during the day when the sun melted the ice. Once again we had to move and resume our other identities.

Angela gave us each a small piece of bread wrapped in cloth and kissed us three times on our cheeks. Doortje and Isabella hugged me. They cried and I cried. I watched them waving until we left and got onto the main road. Angela and her girls had become close friends, and we'd forever be grateful for their goodness. I was still choking back tears as we rode off.

Along the way, I thought about how we left the farm in Ermelo without saying good-bye to the farmer and his family. Would they have cried to see us go? Over the years that followed, I've thought several times about sending them a thank you note, like my mother wanted. But I worry about revealing that we had, in fact, been Jewish refugees. I know how strongly the farmer felt about that.

The people from the Underground said they were taking us to Zwolle, which was more than forty kilometers away, on roads crowded with more refugees. They said that once we got onto the main roads, we'd blend in with everyone else, as we had on our way to the farm a few months before. It was hard to believe I'd experienced so much in so little time.

When the Underground had taken Hannah away, we didn't know where she was being transported. We were to discover, to our amusement and disappointment, that she'd been in Ermelo, the town close to where we stayed with the farmer and his family.

My sister no longer had any need for her cast, and now she was able to rejoin us because the Nazi guards had left. The war was going badly for them and they had bigger problems to deal with. Papa was ecstatic when he heard this news, but didn't tell Mama and me. He wanted it to be a surprise.

CHAPTER THIRTY-TWO
HANNAH JOINS THE JOURNEY

We were back to being refugees, too weak and broken to work. As we rode on the backs of the bicycles, we entered Ermelo. The guard who accompanied us had a gun under his coat. Papa rode on the back of the guard's bike, and Mama and I rode with two women. That way I looked like the son of one and my mother looked like the sister of the other.

We turned down a street, and there in front of us was the hospital. At the entrance stood Hannah! She was standing straight and looked too skinny.

Mama burst into tears and buried her face in the back of the woman riding the bike. Papa had silent tears sliding down his face. I was so happy to see Hannah that I almost blurted out a greeting. All the time we'd been hiding in a nearby farm, Hannah had been so close, and we hadn't known.

The woman riding my bicycle got off and Papa got on. I went to the guard's bicycle and hopped on, taking Papa's place. The woman helped Hannah get on the back of the bicycle behind Papa and watched as Hannah put her arms around our father for the first time in two years. With Hannah hanging on to Papa, we set off down the road to a new hiding place.

Just outside of the town we stopped, got off our bicycles, and gave Hannah big hugs. There was no cast under her coat and she could move normally again. All of us sat on rocks and got reacquainted. I gave her the letter that I had never sent.

Hannah told us about how she'd stayed in bed most of the time. She'd walk around the room during the day to get some exercise and the nurse brought her books to read. The windows were covered, so she never saw sunshine and day blended into night without her ever knowing. There'd been an old Jewish woman, Rifka, in the bed next to Hannah, so they played cards and talked. Rifka was also hiding under the pretense of having a contagious disease. Hannah said the nurse told her Bible stories from the New Testament and tried to convince Hannah to become Christian. At night the old lady next to Hannah told her stories from the Old Testament to keep her Jewish roots firm. Hannah said she felt like she was on a teeter-totter all the time. After a while, whenever the nurse came in, Hannah would pretend to be sleeping.

Soon the cyclists told us we had to be on our way. As I hung on, I thought about how much there was to tell Hannah. It seemed like a lifetime since we'd seen each other. I guess it had been a lifetime—*my* lifetime.

Now there were more people than I could have imagined on the roads. There were horses pulling wagons filled with possessions, and bikes—some with steel and some with wooden rims. People's faces looked like skeletons' faces. Their shoes were falling off, their toes peeked through, touching the snow and ice. These people were searching for food; they'd walked days and nights without sleep to get to their destination, and they were all going to the same city where we were headed.

The city had more chances, everyone thought. When we got closer, we got off the bikes. This group of helpers on bikes would leave us here, but someone would meet us on the other side of the bridge that was just up ahead. Nazis were guarding it, so we'd have to split up and hope for the best. The plan was for us to travel separately and pretend we didn't know each other. That way, if one was detained, the others might still get across.

Our guard talked to a young man waiting in a wagon behind us, then came back to get me. Before saying good-bye, he pushed me up onto the seat beside the driver. For now, I was going to be part of this person's family. I didn't see where Mama, Papa, and Hannah went because I stared straight ahead, afraid for my life. I knew I had to appear relaxed, but my body was stiffening. I gripped the edge of the seat until my knuckles turned white.

The wagon driver looked at me and smiled, trying to reassure me, I think. He asked my name, and I gave him my false identity. He patted my head and told me it would be all right. He clucked to the horses, and we bounced over the cobblestones as we moved forward.

Eventually our wagon passed Mama's, then Papa's, then Hannah's, but we had to look as if we were strangers. Papa and Mama were staring straight ahead. Hannah was squinting and looking around. She was terribly pale from being inside for two years.

As the horses clomped over the stones, the bridge ahead came into view—and so did the Nazis with their rifles. They were looking at identification papers. The man on the wagon told me to let him do all the talking. I was happy to do that! I repeated my false name over and over in my head—*Henk de Jong, Henk de Jong*—and it reminded me again of my playmate Henk, before we had to run. That felt like so long ago.

The soldiers approached and looked in our wagon. They lifted items and looked under seats. When asked, the father said we were from Ermelo and were looking for a place to stay. He swept his arm over all of his family, including me, to show that we weren't harmful. I felt the Nazis' eyes on me. Their harsh words bore into my brain so I kept my eyes lowered. Sitting on my hands, as if trying to keep them warm, was really to stop them from shaking. Finally, one soldier waved his rifle and told us to pass. The wagon lurched forward. I was afraid to look back to see if Mama, Papa, and Hannah had made it through. On the far side of the bridge, the wagon driver gave me a big fatherly smile. At that moment I dared to feel just a little bit safer. It was then that I realized I'd been holding my breath the whole time.

CHAPTER THIRTY-THREE
THE BEGINNING OF THE END

Little did I know then, that there were only two months left until liberty would touch all of us. Zwolle would become the last place I lived before I was able to return to our home in Den Haag and resume a semblance of normal living.

As I jostled along, listening to the clatter of wagons and the voices of people around us, I had a tinge of hope in my heart. I knew I'd still live day to day with fear of the unknown. Even if the war ended and we were able to eventually return to Den Haag, how long would that fear remain with me? And would our home still be there? Had it been bombed? Would my father's store be standing? Would I be able to attend school? Now that I hadn't been in school for so long, I missed it—a little.

When we were far enough from the bridge, we stopped under the shade of some trees near a large brick church and waited for my family to catch up. The stained glass windows had large jagged holes in them, and part of the roof had fallen to the street. Wagons lined the road. People seemed to be living in them. Little grimy-faced children were running around trying to catch each other. I couldn't see any more soldiers. Maybe they'd all gone to fight the advancing Allies and weren't concerned about ragged, starving refugees.

After a heartfelt but hurried reunion, the four of us were taken to an empty row house on the edge of the city. The houses had been abandoned and all the windows and doors were boarded up. We walked around the corner and down a small lane. The backyards of the houses were filled with debris and garbage. Through a heavy door, we entered the back of the one selected for us.

Inside, dark curtains covered all the windows and the front entrance. I could see the wooden frame of the house through holes in the walls. There were mattresses on the floor, and I assumed we'd be sleeping on them. A few tables were set up with mismatched chairs. There was no stove, so once again we'd spend a lot of our time under blankets on worn-out mattresses. Walking around, I found a toilet but no bathtub. The snow would be melting soon, and the days would become warmer, but I knew I'd shiver the whole time we were there.

We were only in this house for one week and were the only family there, so we each had our own mattress. Once a day someone brought small scraps of food such as bread, or pieces of cheese, or raw potatoes, which we ate at night before falling asleep.

We were told this house was used as an arms depot for the Underground, and that guns were hidden in the back room that had a big padlock on the door. People came and went regularly during the nights of that week. They'd slink in, go into the arms room and come out carrying weapons under their coats and in their boots.

Every day a man came and stayed overnight. His name was Fritz. My parents and he would play cards, and I'd be the "fourth man" to make a game until I fell asleep at the table. Then my sister would stop her reading and take my place. Fritz always had his pistol on the table next to the cards he was playing. He was our guard and was there to let people fetch the guns.

Every night my mother would plead with Fritz to take us somewhere else. It was too dangerous to live in a building with live ammunition and guns. There might be an explosion or a raid, and we'd all be killed. She told him we didn't expect a lot, just to be safe. Were there any other places available for hiding?

One night Fritz arrived and told us he was going to take us out of the house, but he had to place us all in different hiding spots. We'd have to be separated because it was just too difficult to find a place with room for four people.

As he was telling us, there was a knock at the door. Fritz held his hand up to signal silence. The knock came again, in a code—one knock and then two short raps. Fritz opened the door and welcomed a young man. They talked in low tones and then Fritz turned to say that the man was there for Hannah. This time there was a small motorbike on the path with a sidecar where Hannah would sit. It was difficult for her to lift her legs to get into the car but once she was settled, the man pushed the bike out into the front street. He started it there so it wouldn't be connected to our house in case it was heard.

The next person to leave was Mama, and she was picked up on a bicycle. Papa would be the last to leave. I climbed onto another bicycle driven by a woman who could've been my mother. She was dressed in a tweed coat with a brown kerchief over her hair. She had black tie-up shoes with small square heels, and I wondered how she could cycle wearing such fancy shoes. I sat on the seat sideways and my feet dangled to one side. My arm was around her waist and the side of my face rested on her back. Papa patted me on the shoulder and said we looked just like a mother and son out for a ride. Then he waved us off and kept waving until we turned the corner.

I'd find out later that my parents moved from place to place every few days to cover their tracks and because there were so many people to hide. This was the first time I'd been apart from Mama and Papa. Could I handle being on my own without my family for support? Did I know what to do and what not to do so I wouldn't betray our situation? I felt the heaviness of responsibility settling on my shoulders. All those years I'd wanted to be grown up. Now that I was, I couldn't be sure I was ready for what maturity demanded of me.

CHAPTER THIRTY-FOUR
LAST LETTER TO OMA

23 March, 1945

Dear Oma,

I hope that this is my last letter to you, Oma, and that we will soon be reunited. I feel very lucky that we have survived this war, and I know in my heart that the end is near.

This could be my last hiding place. The man in this home is like another father. He is so nice to me. His wife can make anything taste good, even if it's made from disgusting things. The man's name is Matthijs. He said I could tell you his real first name because Matthijs is a common name in his city. He laughed when he said the Nazis would have to drag in fifty men to question if my letter was found. Matthijs's wife has rosy cheeks that get rosier when she laughs. How nice it is to hear laughter again!

The family has a big house, which has miraculously escaped damage. We pretend that I am their nephew from Ermelo and have been sent to stay with them by my parents, who had no food and worried that I would die of starvation. I use my fake name and still say it over and over each night so I can answer to it when someone calls.

I have a tiny room in the attic and I'm the only one up there. My bed's a mattress on the floor with four blankets and a quilt because there's no heater. I can see and touch the slats of wood supporting the roof and trace my fingers along the holes in the walls. I feel lucky that the weather is getting warmer, but many mornings I awaken to ice on my pillow where my breath has frozen.

I spend most of my time in the kitchen visiting, or in the sitting room reading, or I'm outside walking around the area. I meet children my age, but usually they've moved on by the time I go back to play a few days later.

Matthijs's home has always been used as a boarding house for adults, and now one of the tenants is a Nazi officer. I don't know the other tenants because they are always gone when I go in for breakfast. And I go to bed before they come home. Whenever I see the officer I lower my eyes and try to pass him without touching.

Oom (uncle) Matts, as I'm supposed to call him, is a hunter and a fisherman. He keeps bees in his backyard. Over the winter, all his tenants had honey on their bread for breakfast. Oom Matts gives me magazines with pictures of sports, hunting, and fishing and says I can cut out the pictures. He's teaching me about what's in the books, and promises he'll take me fishing when the ice melts.

Matts and his wife have a teenage son who's grumpy all the time. He's always glaring at me and is rude when he speaks, so I try not to talk to him. I don't even remember his name.

There's also a daughter who has a job in the city. She has a boyfriend who works on a farm. Sometimes she and I cycle out to see him. We pretend we're just going for a leisurely bike ride, but we always end up at the farm. She and her boyfriend leave me to work with the farmer while they go off somewhere to talk. Helping the farmer brings back memories of my time with the farmers along our road. It's good to be working on a farm again, getting my hands dirty and milking cows, not necessarily in that order. This farmer was surprised at how much I knew.

Mama's very brave letting Hannah and me live somewhere else at our ages. When I left the gun house, she told me that she'd worry about us every night. I think about what Mama said each time the doorknocker bangs. I drop what I'm doing, run to my bed, and crawl under the blankets. Sometimes I run out the back door and hide in the yard until the visitor leaves.

I lie awake many nights hearing the roar of airplanes and the far-off sounds of explosions. I know by now that the Allies have advanced farther into Holland and are turning back the Nazis throughout Europe. Because there are no radios, we depend on the news Matts and his daughter bring home. I hope that what we hear is true and that Allied soldiers will drive out the Nazis. I want to believe, but I'm afraid of being disappointed. When I wake up every morning, I don't know what to expect.

Lying in my bed, I think about Kazimir and Alfred and wonder where they are now. I think about our summer home, and how happy we were for a short while. Sometimes I have dreams without words— just feelings, sounds, and smells. There was one recurring dream about Opa and how he comforted me, even though I don't remember his face very well. In my dream he held me close and I smelled the dampness of his wool sweater, and felt his whiskers on my ear. It felt like he was right there looking after me and comforting me with his warm arms.

In other dreams, I have flashbacks of the backyard in Zwickau and the smell of the black earth. Or I can feel the rocking of that long train ride we took to the Netherlands. One dream was more like a nightmare where I felt panic as I ran and ran into blackness. After that one, I woke up covered in sweat, hoping that I hadn't shouted out and awoken the officer downstairs.

Now, every night as I go to sleep, I try to dream about seeing you again and being reunited with Mama, Papa, and Hannah. I dream about going home.

Your grandson,
Walter

CHAPTER THIRTY-FIVE
LIBERATION

Looking back now, Jenny, I think that staying with that lovely family was the best thing that could have happened to me right then. It eased me into a more trusting frame of mind, so that when the war was over, it wasn't such a shock to me. That experience gave me a hint at a normal life, even though I was answering to Henk instead of Walter and living with strangers. The house was full of warmth from this family and it felt like a haven. I could roam about more freely because of my false identity, and slowly the fear began to subside. I hoped I wasn't being overly confident. I worried about what would happen if there was a raid, or if soldiers found out about me. How would I react if I was feeling too safe?

Janneke, Matts' daughter, turned out to be a secret courier for the Underground. That's how the Underground discovered that her parents would take me into their home. Mama said later that she worried about putting me there because if the Nazis found out about Janneke, my life would be in danger, too. Luckily, Mama didn't know about the Nazi officer who boarded there.

One day in mid-April, I noticed I hadn't seen that officer for a few days and was no longer passing him in the hallway. I didn't dare ask anyone about it. Later that day, Janneke came home early from her job and burst into the house, yelling at the top of her lungs.

"The Allies are coming! The Nazis are gone! We are free!" and she cried and laughed and danced all at the same time. I stood there numbly. My stomach was in knots. I stopped breathing.

Marija, Matts' wife, came from the kitchen wiping her hands on her apron and stood speechless. Her mouth was open but no words came out. After Janneke's outburst, there was complete silence. I felt paralyzed. Doors opened along the hallway and the other tenants timidly stepped out. All of us stared at Janneke. We didn't know whether or not to believe her.

She looked at everyone and opened her arms wide. "It's true, it's true. We're liberated!" she cried.

There was an eruption of cheers, cries of joy, and laughter. Sporadic little dances broke out. At that moment, Matts came running in to tell us the good news and smiled when he saw that we already knew.

"The Canadian tanks are coming over the bridge and going to the town center," he said. "I think we should all go and welcome them."

People swarmed to the door so quickly that I got shoved aside in their haste to leave. People from adjoining houses were streaming out of their homes, running in the streets, cheering and crying. I saw Dutch flags flying behind some of the people, flags that had been hidden away, waiting for a reason to flutter freely once again. Children were on their bikes and elderly people hobbled along supporting each other. Everywhere I looked there were tears, smiles, and joy. There were so many people, more than on a normal day. I saw them emerging from doorways, shielding their eyes from the sun, and holding hands. Gingerly they stepped onto the street, looking left and right, as if they expected to be attacked. I realized they were also *onderduikers*—people who'd been in hiding—just like me.

When I got to the center I saw huge greenish grey tanks with guns on the front. The long barrels were covered in wreaths of flowers as if the city had been anticipating their arrival and had prepared welcoming garlands. Young soldiers were leaning down from the tanks, shaking hands, and accepting kisses. The soldiers on the ground were handing out cigarettes and chocolate. I looked for my family but couldn't see them in the crowds. A soldier bumped into me, and when he saw me, he gave me a cigarette and shook my hand. I put the cigarette in my pocket to give to my father later.

I was surrounded by shouts, sounds of tanks, singing, and laughing. Strangers grabbed me in hugs. The outpouring of joy and relief resulted in my own release of the worst tension and fear anyone could

Jubilant Canadian forces arrived to the cheers of people from all walks of life and suddenly the streets were filled with people, some of whom, like Walter, had been hiding for years.

imagine in a short life. I began to cry. My whole body shook with every sob. Those tears began to wash away the horrors, panic, and helplessness of the last five years. In that boisterous crowd of hundreds, I felt totally alone.

I stood there crying aloud, with my hands by my side and my chest heaving. Moans interrupted sobs. My sweater was getting wet from the tears. The knot in my stomach had turned to nausea and I felt like I was going to be sick from the fumes. Vomit rose in my throat but I swallowed it down.

When I finally looked up I saw a tank beside me. An Allied soldier

Celebrations like this one played out across the Netherlands as Canadian soldiers rolled in on tanks with candy and cigarettes instead of bullets and artillery.

was reaching down to touch my hand. "Hello, my name is Ben. I'm from Canada. What's your name?" He smiled at me.

I grabbed his hand and walked along beside the clanking piece of metal, not knowing how to thank him. I couldn't find words.

"My name is Walter," I sobbed, realizing that I could use my real name again. I fought hard to think of something to say, and then the tank stopped suddenly. Still holding the soldier's hand, I looked up at him. The sun caught a glint of something dangling from his neck. Looking through the tears I could see a prism of color surrounding the object. He was wearing a silver Star of David.

It was April 14, 1945. For us in Zwolle, the war was over.

Epilogue
MAY 8, 1995

My epic letter concludes, and this is the end of my story. Jenny, I am glad that you were never where I was, and I regret that I did not have then what you have now. But I hope you understand.

You're probably wondering what happened next. That day of liberation my family and I reunited and spent the day together. We continued to stay where we'd been hidden, and Oma stayed where she was, until all of Holland was liberated and the formal surrender was signed on May 8, 1945.

Hannah and I returned to school in Zwolle, trying to catch up on our studies in preparation to move back to Den Haag that summer. One day in class I asked for help with a math problem. The teacher said to me, "You should know that. We covered the concept last year; where were you?"

"I was hiding in a hole in the ground!" I cried out.

Hannah had become a young woman while we'd been apart. She seemed more subdued than I remembered. I didn't dare tease her anymore and when I'd look at her, she would smile softly but in a distracted way. She worried about losing so much of her education. Staying behind in Zwolle to finish the school year was important to her.

After the surrender, my parents returned to Den Haag, where they reunited with Oma. The honest butcher handed back the keys to my father's tea and coffee shop, and our belongings that he'd kept safe. Life resumed—although it was vastly different from the life we'd left. Hannah and I joined the family when school ended in Zwolle.

Later, I studied biology, learning more about the insects I'd admired when I was a child. My experiences on farms had instilled in me a love of farming, so agriculture became my area of expertise. I moved to Israel as a young man, and became a teacher of biology. I helped develop a new kibbutz, where I was put in charge of gardening.

We never again saw the members of the Underground who'd helped us survive the time when we were shadows in hiding. We were always grateful to them. Sadly, Opa Bakker was arrested and executed in March, 1945—two months before the liberation.

Henk and I lost touch, but he remains in my heart because of his accepting and sharing nature. Many times I've thought about going back to Nunspeet to see where he is now. Although my memories of living in the summer home were happy, I still cannot reconcile reliving our time of hiding in the Hidden Village. Maybe one day you and I will travel to the village site and pay homage to those who died and those who helped us, in spite of the risks they took. They did whatever it took to keep us safe. They are to be honored forever.

Your loving grandfather,
Walter

This undated photo of Walter was taken shortly after the war. He was always keenly aware that although he had lost his childhood, unlike countless others, he and his family were lucky to have survived the war with their lives.

Author's Note

In 1964, Yad Vashem, the living memorial to the Holocaust, honored Opa Bakker posthumously and Tante Cor as Righteous Among Nations. This is an award given to non-Jews who risked their lives to save Jews from the Nazis in WWII. In 1999, Edouard and Jacoba

von Baumhauer were also honored, posthumously, as Righteous Among Nations. In 1984, the Resistance Memorial Cross, an award given to members of the Dutch Resistance, was presented to Mr. von Baumhauer's widow and Tante Cor. Even though he had passed away, Mr. von Baumhauer eventually got his medal as Walter had hoped.

Mr. von Baumhauer

After liberation, Walter continued his education in The Hague, and in 1949, he went on to study sub-tropical agriculture in Holland. In 1950-51, he studied at the Institute for Jewish Youth Leaders in Jerusalem. He moved to Israel in 1953 and was a member of a kibbutz in Galilee, working as a tractor driver, shepherd, and mentor of young immigrant children, as well as being a leader in the Israeli youth movement. From 1961, he studied and taught biology and did research in Haifa, receiving the Amos de Shalit Prize for science teaching in 1975.

While living in Israel, Walter changed his name to Ze'ev, which means wolf in Hebrew. He married and had two sons. In 1977 he and his family returned to Amsterdam where he taught biology and Hebrew. He has published a book and numerous papers on Dutch Jewish genealogy. Now a widower, Ze'ev lives in his own apartment in Amsterdam, and has two granddaughters who live and study nearby.

Mrs. von Baumhauer

Acknowledgments

Thank you to Ze'ev Bar for telling me your story, painful as it was, in 2008, and for being my friend ever since.

Thank you to Rona Altrows for your support and encouragement as my mentor and friend, and for helping this story become what it is today.

To the students in Nikki Babiuk's grade four class from FFCA in 2011, thank you for listening to my efforts and giving me feedback when I read excerpts to you, after we got all our work done, when I was subbing in your classroom.

Thanks go out to Maude Dahme, Henk Kormelink, and Marja de Bolster for your Hidden Village information and encouragement.

To everyone who helped read, edit, and respond to my ongoing nine-year saga, I appreciate your comments and support: Rachel Black, Barb Howard, Jennifer Wees, Jack Cohen, Jackie and Joyce Robbins, Robin van Eck, Laura Shuler, Linda Reynolds, Mayor Naheed Nenshi, Roland de Jong/Historisch Centrum Overijssel, David Hargrave, Ben and Laurie Minuk, Don Minuk, and Linda Row.

Thank you to Kathryn Cole, my editor, and her team from Second Story Press for making this a true learning experience and the journey of a lifetime.

About the Author

JANET WEES has been writing since she was nine years old. A retired teacher, she spends her time creating children's picture books, reading, walking, writing letters, cycling, volunteering, and traveling. She lives in Calgary, Alberta.

PHOTO CREDITS

Page 9: courtesy of Ze'ev Bar

Page 18 (A): courtesy of Janet Wees

Page 18 (B): courtesy of Ze'ev Bar

Page 29: courtesy of Ze'ev Bar

Page 58: courtesy of Janet Wees

Page 59: courtesy of Janet Wees

Page 61: courtesy of Janet Wees

Page 69: courtesy of William von Baumhauer and Gabrielle De Muralt

Page 94: courtesy of William von Baumhauer and Gabrielle De Muralt

Page 98: courtesy of William von Baumhauer and Gabrielle De Muralt

Page 102: courtesy of Janet Wees

Page 123: courtesy of William von Baumhauer and Gabrielle De Muralt

Page 156: Donald I. Grant / Canada. Ministère de la défense nationale / Bibliothèque et Archives Canada / PA-145972

Page 157: Donald I. Grant / Canada. Ministère de la défense nationale / Bibliothèque et Archives Canada / PA-136176

Page 160: courtesy of Ze'ev Bar

Page 162: courtesy of William von Baumhauer and Gabrielle De Muralt

Page 163: courtesy of William von Baumhauer and Gabrielle De Muralt

Back Cover: courtesy of David Hargrave